TABLE OF CONTENTS

3	INTRODUCTION
4	SUPERHERO'S GUIDE: THE GREAT AWAKENING
14	SUPERHERO'S GUIDE: PROTECTING YOUR ENERGY
19	DISSOLVING YOUR CHAKRAS
27	SUPERHERO'S GUIDE: UNIVERSAL TIME MATRIX
32	SUPERHEROES ARE NEVER VICTIMS
37	FORGIVENESS
41	ZERO POINT
44	EARTH'S CHAKRAS
53	GAMMA RAYS
59	GRIDWORKERS
66	EMERALD TABLETS
69	PLATONIC SOLIDS
78	GALACTIC ZODIAC IMPRINTS
81	TIMELINES
86	LAW OF ONE
90	RECOGNIZING CO-DEPENDENCY
93	AKASHIK RECORDS
96	MORPHOGENTIC CHAKRAS - HIGHER CHAKRAS

TABLE OF CONTENTS

102	8TH CHAKRA
109	9TH CHAKRA
113	10TH CHAKRA
119	ORGONITES
122	11TH CHAKRA
128	12TH CHAKRA
132	13TH CHAKRA
137	14TH CHAKRA
146	15TH CHAKRA
157	GALACTIC HUB HANDSHAKE
163	144 SOUL EXTENSIONS (MONAD)
169	LIGHT BODY SUPERCHARGING
181	UNLOCKING YOUR SUPERPOWERS
186	A MESSAGE FROM THE AUTHOR

Introduction

The Superhero's Guide to Higher Chakras and Light Body Awakening

Prepare to embark on an extraordinary journey that will unlock the true potential of your mind, body, and spirit. Within these pages lies the knowledge of the higher chakras, morphogenic fields, light body activations, harmonic universes, and meditations designed to elevate your consciousness to superhero heights!

This is Part 2 of the **Ascension Classified Intel 5D** books, as well as the **Ascension Navigator Journal**. Read in order for better understanding of terms and concepts. The 12D Shield is crucial to your spiritual evolution.

Morphogenic Chakras :
- The mysterious higher chakras that hold the Blueprint of Your Superpowers.
- Discover the hidden secrets of your morphogenic chakras, the energetic blueprints that hold the key to your unique superpowers.
- These chakras are the portals to higher dimensions, enabling you to access cosmic wisdom and unleash your latent abilities.

Light Body Activations: Igniting Your Inner Star
- Learn how to activate your light body, the radiant vehicle of your soul that transcends time and space.
- Through guided activations and practices, you'll ignite the inner star within you, illuminating your path to ascension and beyond.

Harmonic Universes: Navigating the Cosmic Tapestry
- Venture into the realms of harmonic universes, where dimensions intertwine, and consciousness expands.
- Understand how these cosmic layers influence your reality and how to harness their power to navigate your cosmic journey with precision and grace.

Meditations for Cosmic Heroes: Training Your Super Mind
- Equip yourself with meditative practices designed to strengthen your mental fortitude and align your energetic centers.
- These meditations will train your super mind, enhancing your focus, intuition, and connection to the cosmic currents.

Embrace Your Cosmic Destiny:
- As you delve deeper into this book, you'll uncover the heroic potential that lies within you.
- The journey of the higher chakras and cosmic awakening is not just a path to personal enlightenment, but a mission to serve the greater good. Embrace your cosmic destiny and join the ranks of the awakened heroes who are here to transform the world.

Prepare yourself, for your journey into the higher realms of consciousness and the boundless expanse of cosmic power begins now. Embrace this sacred adventure with an open heart and limitless spirit. May you ascend to unimaginable heights, awakening your true potential, and radiate as a beacon of light, guiding and inspiring all of humanity.

Superhero's Guide to the Great Awakening

During this time of Earth Changes

Often called the End Times, Tribulation, or Great Awakening—humanity and the planet are transforming. Each spiritual tradition has its term for this period:

- Christianity: The Tribulation or the Great Shift.
- Hinduism: Transition from Kali Yuga to Satya Yuga (Golden Age).
- Buddhism: Time of the Dharma's renewal.
- Indigenous Traditions: The Purification Time or Return to Harmony.
- New Age Spirituality: The Ascension or Age of Aquarius.
- Islam: The End of Days or renewal of creation.

This is the one thing all the religions agree on - this period of TIME!

Cosmic Cycle of Evolution
- Imagine a grand superhero cycle that spans thousands of years!
- Some traditions suggest these transformative cycles align with astronomical events like the Precession of the Equinoxes—a cosmic clockwork that takes about 26,000 years to complete.
- You have a front row seat to this event!

Massive Energetic Shift
- A massive shift is happening as we move from the third dimension to the fourth and fifth dimensions.
- Huge infusions of Light are entering Earth, dissolving the veil of separation.
- This transformation is both external and internal, affecting our bodies and the planet.

Cellular Transformation
- On a cellular level, many of you are experiencing profound changes. Your etheric body vibrates at higher frequencies, and your physical body is working hard to catch up.
- This creates a "quickening" within you—accelerating your molecular structure and impacting every part of your body.

Signs of Transformation
- Have you noticed changes in your sleeping patterns, eating habits, or sudden mood swings?
- Relationships may drift, and certain people may leave your life.
- These shifts are signs of deeper changes as you adjust to new energies.

Expansion of Consciousness
- This cellular transformation is propelling you into realms that were once mere potential but are now becoming your reality.
- The fabric of your world is shifting, unfolding before your eyes.

Growing Need for Rest
- Feeling unusually fatigued? It's a clear sign your body and spirit are recalibrating.
- Embrace the rest as part of your superhero journey.

The Superhero's Journey Through Transformation

- Transformation within our bodies is happening on multiple levels.
- Aligning with our inner wisdom triggers cellular memories that activate DNA transformation.

Active Participation
- You are an active participant, not a passive observer.
- This journey isn't about choosing sides—it's about embracing the dynamic process, recognizing your role in evolving your being, and contributing to humanity's broader shift.

Commander of Your Journey
- Just like a spaceship commander takes charge, you are the commander of your transformation.
- Your awareness and proactive engagement steer your course through vast, uncharted territories of change.
- Discover and embrace your multidimensional being.

Choices and Consciousness
- The choices you make and the consciousness you bring determine your path in personal evolution and your contribution to the collective awakening.
- Embrace your role with confidence and curiosity—the universe is vast, and your potential is limitless.

Pivotal Moment in History
- Countless souls chose to be here at this pivotal moment, eager to witness and participate in this monumental transformation.
- We are the brave pioneers, the luminous luminaries, navigating change and contributing to a collective awakening.

Witnessed by the Cosmos
- Our presence here testifies to our collective spirit and profound impact. Benevolent cosmic beings, enlightened extraterrestrials, and celestial entities from across the multiverse have gathered to witness and support humanity's great awakening.

Embrace this extraordinary era of transformation with the heart of a superhero. Your journey is unfolding, and your potential is limitless.

Superhero's Guide to Earth's Great Shift

Earth is undergoing a major event, shifting its position in universal space-time and changing its coordinates and timelines.

Epic Transition
- Earth is moving from the 1st Harmonic Universe (Earth's Field) to the 2nd Harmonic Universe.
- If you're sensing this but couldn't explain it, you're witnessing the Ascension of Earth and its inhabitants firsthand.

Earth Bifurcation
- This transformation represents a split in energetic realities.
- Two paths emerge: one aligned with higher consciousness, love, and unity, and the other rooted in fear, division, and stagnation.
- The planet doesn't physically divide, but humanity moves into different vibrational experiences based on choices, beliefs, and inner work.

2 Distinct Paths Are Emerging
- **Higher Path:** The world feels lighter, more harmonious, with deeper intuition, synchronicities, and a sense of purpose.
- **Resistant Path:** Life may feel chaotic and challenging as old systems collapse.

Gradual Transformation
This process starts subtly but becomes undeniable over time. Each soul follows a path resonating with their evolution, creating growth opportunities.

Ascension Cycle
Earth's collective consciousness is moving through higher frequency bands. The lowest frequency levels (1D, 2D, 3D) are merging into higher frequencies within the next Harmonic Universe. This shift shapes our reality based on thoughts, beliefs, and actions.

- **3D Mindsets:** Those clinging to 3D may feel pressure and discomfort, pushing rapid growth and pattern release. (Materialism)
- **New Harmonic Space:** Aligns with the energetic laws of the 2nd Harmonic Universe, affecting collective consciousness and lifting it into higher frequencies.

Reconnect with Higher Self
In higher timelines, we reconnect with deeper spiritual aspects—Soul, Monad, and Christos essence—shaping our true identity.

Healing and Reclaiming
During Ascension, we reclaim these pieces, often healing as memories from different evolutionary stages surface.

Understanding our Lightbody and Human Energy Field reveals that everything around and within us is made of energy and vibrations. In our Ascension model, we harness the power of the 15 Wave Spectrum of Frequency, aligning with the Universal Rays and our Chakra systems.

This graph illustrates the 15 Wave Spectrum of Frequency (May, 2021)

Each Dimension corresponds with a strand of your DNA.

D1 = 1st Strand
D2 = 2nd Strand
D3 = 3rd Strand

Where do you think 3D originated from?

*Adapted from "EnergecticSynthesis.Com"

Superhero Evolution: Transforming Your Lightbody

- As the planet and the human body evolve, the energy layers in our Auras transform, absorbing Earth's energy and rising to higher dimensions.

Stellar Activations

- Stellar Activations are a natural part of this ascension process.
- When particles in lower dimensions speed up to match higher frequencies, this process opens and merges the energy layers in our Auric Field, breaking down barriers and expanding our consciousness.

Building Your Lightbody

- As you build your lightbody, you may notice changes in your lower chakras as they upgrade.
- Many have observed aurora hues, soft pinks, lavenders, and gentle blues. As these chakras shift, the original colors of red, orange, and yellow fade, symbolizing the dissolution of lower chakra fears.
- Refer to **Ascension Classified Intel** to self-heal and unblock your lower chakras. NO GURU$ needed.

Superpower of Light and DNA Activation

Combining Rainbow Colors
When you mix all the colors of the rainbow as light, you get white light—a magical phenomenon. Each color represents a specific wavelength of visible light, and when they combine, they create pure white light.

- **Prism Magic**
  - Remember playing with prisms as kids?
  - We'd catch sunlight, creating a dazzling rainbow—a piece of magic in our hands!
  - This happens because the prism bends light, a process called dispersion.

Impact of Central Sun
- Imagine the new light from the Central Sun bringing higher energies to Earth, transforming our reality.
- These new frequencies are powerful, driving cellular transformation, upgrading our chakras, and restoring our DNA, activating our light bodies (or crystalline bodies).

Junk DNA: Superhero Potential
- For years, scientists called much of our DNA "junk," thinking it had no function.
- Now, we know it's crucial in regulating our genome, influencing everything from cellular processes to consciousness.

DNA Activation
- As we shift into higher frequencies, dormant DNA strands are being activated.
- This "junk" DNA holds the key to greater potential: heightened intuition, telepathy, and a deeper connection to the universe.
- It's a powerful reservoir of information, awaiting activation.

Spiritual and Physical Gateway
- DNA activation opens a gateway for greater energy flow, healing, and understanding our true essence.
- As Earth's frequencies rise, these hidden abilities become accessible, aligning humanity with its higher, multidimensional self.
- This is not just a biological shift, but a profound spiritual evolution unfolding across the planet.

Embrace the adventure, superhero! By unlocking these DNA codes, you embark on a journey toward a brighter, more enlightened existence.

Unlocking Our Cosmic DNA
Cosmic Blueprint

- Researchers in genetics, quantum physics, and metaphysics are diving into the thrilling idea that dormant strands of DNA are part of our cosmic blueprint for higher consciousness. Imagine these hidden strands as secret codes waiting to unleash superpowers within us!
- Activating this "junk" DNA could be the key to humanity's next epic phase of evolution. It's like discovering a hidden map that leads us to ascend to a higher state of being, tapping into powers and potentials we never knew we had.

Guided by Higher Energies
- These higher energies light our path, guiding us through profound changes and enhancing our spiritual evolution toward a brighter, more harmonious existence.

Universal Time Matrix
- The Universal Time Matrix is a grand structure with five density levels, each containing three groups of frequencies called Spectrums of Frequency. These groups form different reality fields known as Harmonic Universes (HUs), each with unique experiences and perceptions.

Earth's Current Position
- Currently, Earth is in the 1st Harmonic Universe, where our everyday experiences and perceptions take shape. But this is just the beginning! As we ascend through these densities, the veil lifts, revealing higher dimensions and deeper consciousness.

Epic Cosmic Voyage
- Imagine embarking on an epic voyage through the cosmos, exploring new realms in each Harmonic Universe, each more wondrous than the last. Earth is on the brink of an extraordinary transformation, ready to transcend its current boundaries. This journey is about awakening to our full potential and embracing our multidimensional existence.

KEY CONCEPTS/COSMIC VOCABULARY:
- **Collective Consciousness** - Earth's consciousness spans across different densities and interfaces with human consciousness in all Harmonic Universes.
- **Harmonic Universes** - Each Harmonic Universe contains unique layers of the Earth matrix and consciousness levels, creating diverse experiences.
- **5th Harmonic Universe** - Holds primal light and sound fields, the foundational rays for all biological forms.

As we stand at the brink of this incredible shift, let's marvel at the vastness of our potential and the grand adventure ahead. The journey through the Harmonic Universes is a voyage of discovery, unveiling the infinite possibilities of our spiritual evolution.

Harmonic Universe	Dimensions	Earth Matrix Level
1st HU	1D-2D-3D	3 layers of the Earth Matrix
2nd HU	4D-5D-6D	3 layers of the Tara Matrix
3rd HU	7D-8D-9D	3 layers of the Gaian Matrix
4th HU	10D-11D-12D	3 layers of the Aramatena or Aurora Earth Matrix
5th HU	Pre-matter	No planetary body or human forms

This table is designed to help you "INNER-STAND" how each Harmonic Universe aligns with Earth's timelines.

Superhero Journey: Discovering Your Multidimensional Self
Acknowledge Your Multidimensional Existence
- Recognize that your body is a multidimensional powerhouse!
- Visualize yourself feeling the different dimensions of your being and their connection to planetary consciousness.
- This journey extends far beyond the 7 basic lower chakras.

Superhero Meditation: Activate Your Multidimensional Powers

Prepare for Your Epic Journey – Find a quiet space, sit comfortably, and take a few deep breaths. Imagine you're suiting up for an exciting adventure into your inner cosmos.

Step 1: Ignite Your Inner Light
- Close your eyes and visualize a bright light at your center, like your superhero power core.
- Feel this light growing stronger, expanding outward, filling you with energy and power.

Step 2: Connect with Your Multidimensional Self
- Imagine this light reaching out to different dimensions, connecting you with your higher self.
- Visualize yourself standing on a bridge between worlds, feeling the energy flow through you.

Step 3: Engage with Cosmic Waves
- Picture yourself riding waves of energy in an ocean of universal consciousness.
- Feel the ebb and flow of these waves, guiding you and enhancing your powers.

Step 4: Reflect and Record
- As the light and energy settle, reflect on your experience.
- Note any sensations, thoughts, or visions in your superhero journal.
- This will be your reference for future cosmic adventures.

Superhero's Guide to Multidimensional Mastery

Channeling Higher Frequencies
- As we focus on understanding our Multidimensionality, we channel our energies into higher frequencies, operating on levels beyond our regular conscious mind.
- 12D Shielding is highly recommended daily while operating in higher chakras. Referenced in my previously published books:
    - *Ascension Classified Intel 5D book*
    - *5D Navigator Ascension Journal*
- When we start to perceive Multidimensionality, our consciousness extends beyond the limitations of our third-dimensional identity, opening us to a greater reality.

Cosmic Adventure
- This journey is like embarking on a cosmic adventure, where we explore the depths of our true selves and connect with the vast energies of the universe.
- Embrace this experience and let your consciousness soar to new heights, discovering boundless potential within!

Connecting Chakras and Mind Matrix
- Many in the New Age community are familiar with the first seven primary chakras—the energy centers we are born within the first density.
- Let's take an exciting step further by linking each of these chakra layers to the levels of the mind matrix within each chakra pattern.

Intelligent Mind Matrix
- The mind matrix is an intelligent force, intricately connected to each chakra, recording its unique characteristics and attributes.
- By understanding this connection, you can align your chakras with the mind matrix, enhancing your energetic signature and deepening your spiritual journey.

Enlightening Journey
- Imagine this process as an enlightening journey where each chakra acts as a gateway or portal, unlocking higher levels of consciousness and energy.

- Embrace your superhero journey through Multidimensionality, channel higher frequencies, and unlock your true potential.

Spiritual Bodies are Conciousness	
1D Frequency	Root
2D Frequency	Sacral
3D Frequency	Solar Plexus
4D	Heart
5D	Throat
6D	Third Eye
7D	Crown

Why do you think Earth has been referred to as 3D?

Superhero Chakra Adventure

Visualize and Amplify
- As you focus on each chakra, visualize it resonating with the mind matrix. Feel your energy amplify, connecting you to the greater universal flow.

Embrace the Adventure
- Each step brings you closer to the harmony and balance of your multidimensional self.

Journey with Curiosity
- Embark on this journey with an open heart. Discover the profound interconnectedness of your chakras and the mind matrix, illuminating your path to the highest potential.
- Unlock your superhero potential and soar to new heights on this exciting adventure!

Sphere / Color Octave	Dimension	Chakras
Chakra 1	D-1	Root
Chakra 2	D-2	Sacral
Chakra 3	D-3	Solar Plexus
Chakra 4	D-4	Heart
Chakra 5	D-5	Throat
Chakra 6	D-6	Third Eye
Chakra 7	D-7	Crown
Chakra 8	D-8	Thymus (Permanent Seed Atom)
Chakra 9	D-9	Thalamus (Medula Oblangata)
Chakra 10	D-10	Galactic - Soul Star (6" above the head)
Chakra 11	D-11	Galactic (10" above head)
Chakra 12	D-12	Earth Star (6" below feet)
Chakra 13	D-13	Earth - Christ 12D Shield (12" Below feet)
Chakra 14	D-14	Universal (36" above head)
Chakra 15	D-15	Universal (beneath Earth)

Superhero's Guide to Protecting Your Energy

Fallen Angelics and Imposter Spirits
These dark forces can be human or non-human spirits, often separated from their souls or never having inhabited a human body. They are lower spirit beings, not powered by divine energy, and can't exist in higher realms. If humans aren't mentally clear and emotionally balanced, they can become possessed by these spirits, leading to misery and agony.

Risks and Protection
- **Stage One Risk**: Reckless behavior and indulging in negative emotions like fear, guilt, and shame put you at risk. Stay disciplined and aware to avoid this.
- **Stage Two Risk**: Being in a trance, obsessive thoughts, or constant exposure to technology disrupts your energy field. Shield yourself with meditation and awareness.
- **Stage Three Risk**: Addictions (drugs, alcohol, etc.) and psychoactive drugs can change brain function and increase risk. Practice moderation and seek healthier alternatives.
- **Stage Four Risk**: Promiscuous sexual activity and using pornography create vulnerabilities. Maintain healthy relationships and clear intentions.
- **Stage Five Risk**: Deviant behaviors like pedophilia and sadism are controlled by dark forces. Avoid these actions to stay clear of such entities.

Building Your Superhero Aura
Strengthen your auric field through meditation, building energy, and stopping leaks.

Maintain awareness and use your 12D shield during transitional states:
- Giving Birth: Protect mother and baby.
- Death Transition: Shield during the passage.
- Sexual Activity: Protect your energy.
- Injuries: Guard against loss of consciousness.
- Group Meditation: Shield in group settings.
- Hospital Visits: Protect against drugs and anesthesia.
- New Places: Shield in unfamiliar environments.
- Traumatic Events: Use shielding during high-stress times.
- Stay vigilant, Superhero! Strengthening your energy field and maintaining awareness will keep you protected from these dark forces and vulnerabilities.

*** Refer to my 1st book for my 12D shield meditation: Ascension Classified Intel.*

Superhero Guide: Mastering Your Senses and Energy

Hearing Superpowers
- **Right Ear**: Your right ear tunes into mental planes 3D, 6D, and 9D. It's like having a super scanner for these dimensions.
- **Left Ear**: Your left ear picks up broadcasts from the astral plane (4D, 7D, and 10D). Be aware, fallen entities might send messages this way. By healing your left side, you can block out the astral interference and tune into your Avatar Christ self, communicating directly through the 10th dimension.

Breathing Superpowers
- **Right Nostril**: Breathing through your right nostril boosts physical energy and balances metabolism. It activates the left (thinking) side of your brain.
- **Left Nostril**: Breathing through your left nostril activates the right (feeling) side of your brain.

Balanced Breathing: Alternate your breaths to access and balance both sides of your brain, ensuring full brain activation. Clear any blockages with breathwork and meditation.

Superhero Brain Balance Adventure
- Prepare for Your Superpower Boost.
- Get into a comfortable seated position, relax your shoulders, and close your eyes. Imagine you're about to embark on an epic adventure to power up your superpowers!

Step 1: Power Up with Right Nostril Breathing
- Imagine your right nostril is the gateway to your superpower energy boost.
- Close your left nostril with your left thumb.
- Inhale deeply through your right nostril, feeling energy surging into your body.
- Hold your breath for a moment, letting the energy build.
- Exhale slowly through your right nostril, releasing any tension.
- Repeat this for 5 breaths, visualizing your superhero suit powering up with each breath.

Superpower Boost: *this energizes your body and mind, activating the left (thinking) side of your brain.*

Step 2: Power Up with Left Nostril Breathing
- Imagine your left nostril is the gateway to calming and balancing superpowers.
- Close your right nostril with your right thumb.
- Inhale deeply through your left nostril, feeling a wave of calmness wash over you.
- Hold your breath for a moment, letting the calm energy settle.
- Exhale slowly through your left nostril, releasing any stress.
- Repeat this for 5 breaths, visualizing your superhero senses sharpening with each breath.

Superpower Boost: *This calms your body and mind, activating the right (feeling) side of your brain.*

Step 3: Balance with Alternate Nostril Breathing
- Imagine alternating nostrils as activating your full superhero potential.
- Close your right nostril with your right thumb and inhale through your left nostril.
- Close your left nostril with your right ring finger and exhale through your right nostril.
- Inhale through your right nostril.
- Close your right nostril and exhale through your left nostril.
- Repeat this cycle for 5 breaths, visualizing a perfect balance of energy and focus.

Superpower Boost: *This balances both hemispheres of your brain, bringing harmony and clarity, readying you for your next adventure.*

Congratulations, Superhero! You've successfully powered up and balanced your brain.

Superhero Insight: Safe People and Healthy Boundaries
Recognizing Safe People:
- To identify Safe People and relationships, we need to understand what makes someone safe and why it's essential for overcoming fear.
- We need honest people who help us improve without condemning us, accepting us while being truthful about our weaknesses.

Avoiding Destructive Relationships:
- Relationships that use shame, guilt, or condemnation are destructive and prevent growth. Unsafe people demand we change to be accepted and loved conditionally.
- Instead, we must become the safe person we need and attract similar people by clearing fears and improving our character.

Qualities of Safe People:
- Are fully present and connect deeply
- Speak truth without offense
- Encourage growth and highest potential
- Create positive, loving relationships

Establishing Inner Safety:
To heal and overcome fears, we must establish safety within ourselves by:
- Taking care of our body
- Practicing meditation or spirituality
- Avoiding self-harming behaviors
- Managing fear and trauma reactions

Setting Healthy Boundaries:
- Enhance inner safety by setting healthy boundaries, especially in draining situations.
- Notice how certain people affect you and connect with your inner compassionate witness.
- Fortify your personal shield with love and positivity, recognizing necessary actions to maintain peace.
- When dealing with such people, we need strong boundaries and clear terms of interaction. In some cases, we may need to sever the connection entirely.
- Continuously feeding destructive, harmful, or abusive relationships that won't heal or evolve is unproductive.

Planting Seeds of Growth:
- To nurture a positive environment, plant seeds where there is fertile soil. Sometimes, this means pulling weeds or walking away from unhealthy relationships as an act of self-love and self-preservation.

Superhero Upgrade: Exciting Changes in Our Chakra System and Planetary Evolution

Epic Chakra and Planetary Shift
Our chakra system is deeply influenced by the planets, and right now, an exciting shift is happening. Let's dive into the details:

Saturn's Influence and Breaking Free
- Saturn's influence on the root chakra has caused thoughts of survival and victimization, thanks to mind control.
- This area is now undergoing significant changes, especially for those on the healing path. We're breaking free from these manipulative influences.

AI Mind Control Overlay
- An AI mind control overlay has been affecting our chakras, sending harmful frequencies to suppress and manipulate us.
- This is part of a larger agenda to create a master-slave dynamic and increase cycles of victimization.

Gaining Clarity and Freedom
- Good news! We're gaining clarity and breaking free from Saturn-directed mind control as we move toward higher, ascending timelines.
- The lower energy fields and low frequencies of the root chakra are dissolving for those on the ascension path, merging into a single energy column.

Freedom from Victim-Victimizer Cycle
- This shift offers potential freedom from the victim-victimizer cycle controlled by Saturn's influence.
- We're discovering that certain planetary influences, especially negative ones, have affected our chakra system without most people being aware.

Collective Fields and Soul Timelines
- The collective fields of the planet are moving into the soul timelines of the fourth, fifth, and sixth-dimensional fields of the next Harmonic Universe.
- For those who haven't dissolved their chakra membranes, the fourth, fifth, and sixth-dimensional wave spectrum will gradually replace and connect to the lower energy centers where the first, second, and third chakras previously existed.
- Embrace this superhero journey and the exciting changes ahead. Break free, gain clarity, and unlock your true potential!

Superhero Evolution: Embodying the Soul Matrix

Soul Matrix Embodiment
- The Soul matrix is fully embodying in the core of the human body, removing barriers between the solar plexus and heart.
- Many are shedding the old lower chakra configurations.
- This planetary event is transforming the chakra energy center configuration based on spiritual integration and genetic arrangement.

Embrace the Transformation
- These changes bring us toward greater freedom, clarity, and spiritual evolution.
- As we navigate these shifts, we unlock our potential and align with higher, more harmonious timelines.
- Embrace this journey with excitement, knowing each step brings us closer to our true, multidimensional selves.
- The future is bright, and we are on the path to profound transformation and awakening.

Exciting Shifts in Lower Body Energies
- Feel a buzz in your lower body energies?
- Our lower chakras (1D-2D-3D) are getting a major upgrade!
- We're being flooded with higher energy frequencies that match the larger planetary shifts.
- As Earth's energy grids evolve, so does our body's energy structure, transforming our spiritual energy patterns.

Ascension Symptoms and Energetic Reconnections
- While these changes might bring ascension symptoms, they are powerful energetic reconnections.
- These higher frequencies tune our glandular system and organs linked to the lower chakras, enhancing our physical and spiritual well-being.

Shifting into the 2nd Harmonic Universe
- We're transitioning into the dazzling 2nd Harmonic Universe!
- For those on the ascending path, this means moving into higher realms of consciousness, while others might remain or descend within the third-dimensional timeline on 3D Earth.

Coexisting Timelines
- Both groups—those ascending and those staying in 3D—coexist on the planet but at different points in the time-space continuum.

It's a wild ride: Keep your hands in until it comes to a complete stop.

Superhero Transformation: Exciting Chakra Upgrades

Unifying Your Chakra Column
- You're starting to unify your chakra column into one powerful light field (Hara line).
- This needs to happen to embody the higher morphogenetic chakras and frequencies.
- The membranes between your chakras dissolve, forming a single, unified light channel.
- This doesn't happen overnight and requires inner work—no hired guru can do it for you.

Transcend the Frequency Fence
- This incredible transformation aligns your light body with planetary fields and beyond, allowing you to transcend Earth's vibrational Frequency Fence and break free from the cycle of reincarnation.

Multidimensional Understanding
- Our spiritual evolution is intertwined with understanding our multidimensional anatomy.
- As we grow, we become more aware of our interconnected spiritual, mental, and physical selves.
- Even if the details seem overwhelming, focusing on your higher spiritual levels brings profound miracles.

Transforming Chakra Colors
- As part of our divine journey, we'll eventually recode the colors of our lowest chakras.
- The red wave spectrum, linked to negative emotions like anger and fear, will become obsolete.
- These lower frequencies will be replaced by higher-vibrating colors like greens, blues, and pastels, forming the new foundation of our spiritual bodies.

I remembered when this started happening to me - I thought I broke my chakras. My chakras began dissolving colors into a lavender and pink from the Root Chakra up.

Embrace the Future
- This exciting transformation is part of our ascension journey.
- By clearing negative energies and embracing higher frequencies, we evolve spiritually and align with our true multidimensional selves.
- This journey is filled with wonder and discovery, leading us to a more harmonious and enlightened existence.

I'm writing this to encourage you to embrace these changes!!

Space Adventure Meditation: Clearing Chakra Blockages with Laser Beams!

Prepare for Launch
- **Center Yourself:** Strap in and find a quiet, comfortable space. Close your eyes, take a few deep breaths, and feel your body relax as you prepare for lift-off.

Set Your Course
- **Heart Chakra Focus:** Shift your awareness to the heart chakra, located in the center of your chest. Feel its warmth and love, like the glowing core of your spaceship.
- **Hara Line Connection:** Visualize a bright line of light running vertically through your body—this is your hara line. Follow this light beam as it guides your ship through each chakra, one by one.

Engage Chakras in Perfect Alignment
- **Root Chakra:** Located at the base of your spine, like the stabilizing thrusters of your ship. If it feels off-center, use your intention to realign it.
- **Sacral Chakra:** Just below your navel, like the navigation system. Ensure it is aligned with gentle awareness.
- **Solar Plexus Chakra:** Above your navel, like the power core. Make sure it's balanced and in harmony.
- **Heart Chakra:** Confirm it's glowing brightly at the center, like the ship's reactor core.
- **Throat Chakra:** At your throat, like the communication system. Align it with clarity and truth.
- **Third Eye Chakra:** Between your eyebrows, like the ship's sensors. Bring it into alignment with your intuition.
- **Crown Chakra:** At the top of your head, like the antenna connecting you to the cosmic network. Align it with divine energy from above.

Activate Laser Beams!
- If you detect any blockages, visualize shooting colorful laser beams from your ship, clearing and balancing the energy. Feel the smooth flow of energy from the base of your spine to the top of your head, like your ship gliding effortlessly through space.

Embrace Your Evolution
- Know that aligning your chakras is essential for your spiritual evolution. This alignment boosts your energy flow, propelling you forward with greater clarity and purpose.
- **Personal Responsibility** Remember, the power to align and unblock your chakras is in your hands. This journey of growth and self-discovery is yours to embrace with confidence and trust in your abilities.
- **Complete Your Mission:** When you're ready, take a few more deep breaths, and slowly open your eyes. Reflect on the balance and harmony you've achieved, like a seasoned space explorer returning home from an epic adventure.

Enjoy your journey, Space Guardian!

Keep your chakras in perfect alignment and your spaceship on course for the stars!

Superpowered Journey: Integrating Lower Chakras for Light Body Activation

Get ready, superhero! It's time to harness the power of your lower chakras and activate your light body, unlocking incredible superpowers along the way.

Energy Flow
- Think of your lower chakras as the power generators of your superhero suit. They support the energy flow up through your entire chakra system. If these chakras are blocked or unbalanced, it disrupts your energy flow, making it challenging to fully activate your light body and unleash your superpowers.

Solid Foundation
- These lower chakras provide the solid foundation for your spiritual growth. Without integrating them, the higher chakras (your ultimate power boosters) might not be as effective or stable. It's like building your superhero headquarters on a shaky foundation—not good!
- Complete Transformation.
- Full activation of the light body involves aligning and balancing all chakras, ensuring a holistic and complete transformation. This is where you become the ultimate superhero!

Grounding Force
- Think of your lower chakras as the grounding force connecting you to Earth's energy, helping you navigate the challenges of the physical world. Balanced lower chakras manifest as fearlessness, confidence, and a sense of purpose. You become grounded, centered, and empowered, able to flow through life with superhero-level confidence and clarity.

Next Phase of Evolution
- As you prepare for the next phase of your spiritual evolution, focusing on your lower chakras is essential. This groundwork allows the higher chakras to open, activating your soul's higher wisdom, intuition, and divine connection.
- Balancing these energy centers creates the stability needed to move forward into the higher frequencies of ascension, unlocking your full potential and guiding you toward the highest expression of yourself and light body activation.

Superpowers Unleashed

- As your chakras become open, healthy, and unblocked, you will notice superpowers emerging:
    - **Self-Healing**: Accelerated healing powers.
    - **Age Regeneration**: The ability to maintain youthful vitality.
    - **Enhanced Intuition**: Superhuman insight and wisdom.
    - **Incredible Confidence**: The courage to face any challenge.
- Embrace this journey, superhero! By integrating and balancing your lower chakras, you unlock the full spectrum of your superpowers, ready to take on the world with clarity, confidence, and cosmic strength. (Cape optional, superpowers mandatory!)

I love turning meditations into exciting "field trips"! They should never be boring or painful—imagine them as magical adventures that captivate the attention of your inner child, making every moment feel like a joyful exploration of the cosmos.

As cosmic beings, we have the potential to journey beyond the ordinary, embracing the vastness of our existence for true ascension. These meditation field trips allow us to reconnect with our infinite selves, aligning with the universe's rhythms. Embrace the adventure, let your inner superhero shine, and ascend to new heights of spiritual evolution.

Together, let's transform meditations into exhilarating voyages, tapping into the boundless energy that flows through our cosmic essence.

BALANCING CHAKRA CRYSTALS:

Super Seven is a remarkable crystal known for its ability to balance and harmonize all seven chakras at once. It's also known as "Sacred Seven" or "Cosmic Seven" because it contains seven different minerals: Amethyst, Clear Quartz, Smoky Quartz, Lepidocrocite, Goethite, Rutile, and Cacoxenite. Here's how it can help:

Benefits of Super Seven

- **Energy Alignment**: Super Seven's unique combination of minerals helps align and balance all your chakras, promoting overall energetic harmony.
- **Spiritual Growth**: It enhances spiritual awareness and intuition, making it a powerful tool for meditation and connection with higher consciousness.

- **Emotional Healing:** This crystal supports emotional healing by clearing blockages and promoting a sense of peace and well-being.
- **Protection and Grounding:** Super Seven provides protection against negative energies while grounding your energy in the present moment.
- **Enhanced Healing:** It amplifies the healing properties of other crystals and can boost your own healing capabilities.

How to Use Super Seven for Chakra Balancing
- **Meditation:** Hold the crystal or place it on your body while meditating. Visualize the energy from the Super Seven flowing through all your chakras, clearing and balancing them.
- **Carrying:** Keep the crystal with you throughout the day to maintain balanced energy.
- **Sleep:** Place the crystal under your pillow or beside your bed to promote healing and balance while you sleep.
- **Crystal Grids:** Use Super Seven in crystal grids to amplify its balancing and healing energies.

I use Super7 as my main grid crystal occasionally to FIRE up my grid. Super7 is a powerful amplifier. I also keep a 5 lb (not a typo - 5 lbs) raw peacock ore on my nightstand beside my bed. It's another favorite of mine. It's too large and heavy to carry around and helps balance my chakras while I'm sleeping.

Super 7

Peacock Ore

Superhero Guide: The Universal Time Matrix

Universal Time Matrix
- Imagine a cosmic grid with five density levels, each holding three-dimensional holographic fields.
- These groups of three frequencies form platforms of consciousness and expression, known as Harmonic Universes (HUs).
- Each HU has unique characteristics, resulting in different matter forms and consciousness perceptions.

Stations of Identity
- For human beings, consciousness bodies exist throughout these densities as aspects of the higher self and Lightbody, called Stations of Identity.
- Each Station of Identity is like a superhero version of yourself existing at different levels of consciousness, all contributing to your multidimensional being.
- Every expression of the God source, whether in a collective consciousness body or individual life form, has many Stations of Identity across different dimensions or Harmonic Universes.
- To unify with the God source, we must live in harmony with natural laws.

This harmony helps us integrate, heal, and unify all our spiritual expressions, learning from life lessons and evolving.

Harmonic Universes Breakdown

First Harmonic Universe (1D-2D-3D):
- **Personality Matrix:** The three layers of the personality matrix or incarnated human.

Second Harmonic Universe (4D-5D-6D):
- **Soul Matrix:** The three layers of the soul matrix.

Third Harmonic Universe (7D-8D-9D):
- **Monadic Matrix:** The three layers of the monadic matrix.

Fourth Harmonic Universe (10D-11D-12D):
- **Christos Avatar Matrix:** The three layers of the Christos Avatar matrix.

Fifth Harmonic Universe (13D-14D-15D):
- **Rishi Matrix:** The Three Layers of the Rishi matrix or Threefold Founder Flame.

Harmonic Universe	Dimensions	Earth Matrix Level
1st HU	1D-2D-3D	3 layers of the Earth Matrix
2nd HU	4D-5D-6D	3 layers of the Tara Matrix
3rd HU	7D-8D-9D	3 layers of the Gaian Matrix
4th HU	10D-11D-12D	3 layers of the Aramatena or Aurora Earth Matrix
5th HU	Pre-matter	No planetary body or human forms

Embark on this superhero journey through the Universal Time Matrix, unlocking the secrets of your Stations of Identity and ascending through the Harmonic Universes!

Superhero Adventure: Navigating Timelines and Dimensional Octaves

Holographic Structure of Harmonic Universes
- In the creation of the Harmonic Universes, each dimensional octave has two timelines. For example, in our 3D Earth Harmonic Universe, which consists of dimensions 1D-3D, there are six timelines.

Evolving Through Higher Frequencies
- As we evolve and move up in frequency, we encounter more dimensional octaves and, therefore, more potential timelines.
- These future timelines contain Stations of Identity—our soul, oversoul, higher self—comprising parts of our spiritual bodies that we need to reclaim during timeline collapses in the Ascension cycle.

Healing and Integration
- Those on the spiritual ascension path experience energetic healing by facing cellular memories from different stages of evolution in multiple timelines.
- This process is key to becoming multidimensional.

Reclaiming Identity and Spiritual Growth
- We must move through timelines in each dimensional octave, reclaiming our identity while recoding and transforming obsolete, false timelines.
- This prevents false realities from interfering with our spiritual growth.

Superhero Evolution: Accelerated Planetary Shift

Accelerated Evolution
- Since the original 5D plan couldn't be achieved, our planetary evolution had to speed through various time fields, navigating many inorganic timelines in the Harmonic Universes where Earth has histories and memories.
- This drastic acceleration impacts our experience of time.

Amplified Polarities
- This acceleration amplifies the world's forces, drastically increasing polarities on Earth.

Polarity Integrators
- Many of us have been called to serve Earth as Polarity Integrators.
- These superheroes help balance and harmonize polarities, ensuring smoother transitions through these amplified energies.

Superhero Journey: Ascending Through Timelines

Reclaiming Your Spiritual Body
- When you reclaim your spiritual body and its identity from obsolete or false timelines, you move through these timelines into higher dimensional octaves, continuing to evolve up the spiral of time.
- As we ascend, we become conscious of future time, moving forward in time with each dimensional octave.
- Have you noticed how time is moving rapidly?

Planetary Ascension Cycle
- The planetary Ascension cycle marks the end of the 3D combined timeline, propelling Earth and humanity into a higher frequency of future time, a new dimensional octave with higher frequencies.

Individual Spiritual Evolution
- People on 3D Earth are at different levels of spiritual evolution. Where your frequency stabilizes will determine your direction and future.
- If you embody your Soul Matrix bodies (4D-5D-6D) and enter the next Harmonic Universe, you'll access another potential six timelines (6D = 12 timelines in total).

Reclaiming Timelines

Reclaim and Recoding Timelines
- We must move through timelines in each dimensional octave, reclaiming our identity and recoding false realities that hinder our spiritual growth.
- Are you actively collapsing timelines? Set your intentions to the highest timeline and collapse all lower timelines by speech. This should be done every morning.

Clear Past Issues
- If we don't resolve past issues in our timeline, we repeat patterns until we learn the lesson or clear the original trauma. Everything repeats in a person's timeline until the spirit resolves the energetic conflict.

Change the Timeline
- By clearing and changing the past timeline in the present moment, we alter the current timeline, creating a new future direction. When we clear the past, we move outside the trauma timeline, changing the future and altering the cycle of time.

Superhero Code: Our Actions, Our Results

Energy Quality
- The energy we align with, whether positive or negative, shapes our actions and results.

Discern Organic vs. Inorganic
- Learn to distinguish between natural and artificial forces influencing our lives.

Positive Actions
- Positive actions bring positive results. Focus on deeds that generate happiness, peace, and fulfillment.

Negative Actions
- Negative actions bring negative results. Recognize and clear negative behaviors to break harmful cycles.

Heart and Intuition
- Use your heart to guide decisions, ensuring actions align with positive forces.

Responsibility
- Accept responsibility for your actions. Blaming others only perpetuates negativity.

Change and Growth
- Plant seeds of positive change and nurture them for a brighter future.
- Harness your superhero powers, take positive actions, and watch the ripple effect of good results and blessings!

Superhero Transformation: Inner Child Healing

Inner Child Healing
- This process involves connecting with and nurturing the part of yourself that experienced unmet needs, traumas, or emotional wounds during childhood.

Why It's Necessary
- Emotional Wholeness.
- Healing your inner child helps integrate past experiences, leading to emotional wholeness and stability. This strengthens your emotional resilience and self-awareness.
- Emotional Balance: Achieve emotional stability and resilience.
- Empowerment: Overcome limiting beliefs and unlock your potential.
- Inner child healing helps you reclaim your personal power. By addressing and nurturing past traumas, you start to see yourself not as a victim of circumstances, but as a resilient survivor capable of overcoming challenges.

Overcoming Limiting Beliefs
- Childhood traumas and unmet needs often create limiting beliefs and patterns that hinder personal growth. By addressing these, you break free from self-imposed limitations.

Self-Love and Compassion
- Embracing your inner child fosters self-love and compassion, crucial traits for personal empowerment and connecting with others on a deeper level.
- Inner child work boosts self-esteem and self-worth. As you nurture and love your inner child, you build a stronger, more positive self-image, making it easier to stand up for yourself and reject the victim role.

Empowered Decision-Making
- With a healed inner child, your decisions are driven by confidence and clarity rather than fear and insecurity. This empowers you to take bold actions aligned with your true self.
- With a healed inner child, your decisions become more empowered and intentional. You learn to set healthy boundaries, assert your needs, and make choices that support your well-being, steering clear of the victim mentality.
- The inner child is a wellspring of creativity and joy. Healing this aspect of yourself unlocks these qualities, enriching your life experience.

Enhanced Relationships
- Healing past wounds improves your relationships, as you communicate more authentically and build healthier connections with others.
- Sharing intimacy requires emotional openness and vulnerability. Many fear being hurt, betrayed, or rejected, leading to communication blocks and a shut-down heart. These fears exist in all types of relationships, exacerbating victim-victimizer cycles.

Victim and Victimizer
- As victims, we may feel unlovable or rejected, and as victimizers, we close off emotional vulnerability to protect ourselves. This creates a mask, making us hurt others before they can hurt us.

Access to Creativity and Joy
- The inner child is a wellspring of creativity and joy. Healing this aspect of yourself unlocks these qualities, enriching your life experience.

Emotional Healing
- By addressing and healing emotional wounds, you release pent-up negative emotions like anger, fear, and sadness. This emotional cleansing frees you from the grip of past pains that contribute to a victim mindset.

Yearning for Connection
- We all crave deep, intimate connections to be seen and acknowledged at the core of our inner spirit. This longing reflects our desire to share our deepest truth and be recognized for who we truly are.

Ascension Path
- These spiritual reflections are most intensely felt on our Ascension path, especially when we encounter soul family and monadic mates. Fearless intimacy forms the foundation for these profound connections.

People that constantly discuss past events (bad marriages, childhood events, jobs, relationships...) continue to live in the past and in the drama instead of healing and letting go. I'm not saying the event didn't traumatize you, I'm saying to acknowledge it, release it and live in the present. You should never allow an event to define you or TAKE YOUR POWER.

Superhero Power: The Gift of Forgiveness
Forgive to Free Yourself
- Forgiveness is the greatest gift you can give yourself.
- By forgiving others, you break free from the chains of resentment, anger, and judgment.
- This liberates you from emotional pain and opens your heart.

Heal Your Anger
- Anger harms your brain and closes your heart.
- Forgiving yourself for holding onto anger is essential to breaking free from self-sabotaging victimhood.

Live in the Present
- Understanding the importance of forgiveness brings you into the present moment.
- It helps you move beyond past hurts and embrace open-mindedness and free thinking.

Stay Balanced: Mind, Body, and Spirit
Multidimensional Being
- You are a spiritual being with a body, mind, emotions, and spirit.
- Pay attention to which areas need more care and balance rest with activity.
- Begin journaling to chart your growth and monitor your ascension.
- Explore new activities that embrace your ascension.
- Work with you inner child on healing aspects of your life that need attention.
- Spend more time in nature, gardening and with animals.

Growth and Awareness
- Keep growing your self-awareness and consciousness.
- Stay open to new activities and ideas, while also allowing time for rest and relaxation.

Empower Your Brain and Nervous System
Open Your 12DShield
- Call upon Krystal Star Guardians or guiding beings.
- Command Your Brain and Nervous System.
- Accept only truthful, organic messages.
- Support your higher good and Divine Blueprint.
- Eliminate harmful artificial intelligence messages.
- Evict inorganic or intrusive scripts.
- You are SOVERIGN AND FREE.

Remember, true superheroes find strength in forgiveness, freeing themselves from the chains of the past to embrace a brighter future!

Superhero Insight: The Cycle of Profit

Big Pharma and Doctors
- Some pharmaceutical companies and healthcare providers may exploit patients' past traumas and ongoing struggles for financial gain. By continually focusing on these events, they can keep patients dependent on medications and treatments, ensuring a steady stream of revenue.

Perpetuating Dependency
- Instead of empowering patients to heal and move forward, this approach can create a cycle of dependency. Patients may feel trapped in their pain, constantly revisiting past events without finding true resolution.

Financial Motivation
- The financial incentives for pharmaceutical companies and some healthcare providers can overshadow the genuine need for patient healing. This can lead to over-prescription of medications and unnecessary treatments.

Breaking Free
- True healing involves addressing the root causes of trauma and empowering individuals to reclaim their lives. By focusing on holistic and integrative approaches, you can break free from the cycle of dependency and find lasting wellness.
- Authentic healing lies in acknowledging the past but not letting it define your present or future. Harness your inner power, let go of what no longer serves you, and soar towards a brighter, stronger you!

Remember, your superhero journey involves taking control of your health and well-being and prioritizing your healing and empowerment.

Superhero Power: Forgiveness, Kindness, Compassion, and Self-Love

Choose Your Response
- You hold the power to choose forgiveness, kindness, compassion, and self-love in every moment. By choosing how you respond to yourself and others, you shape your reality.

Free Yourself
- Forgiving others for perceived wrongs liberates you from the chains of judgment, resentment, and anger. It's the most generous gift you can give yourself.

Heal Your Heart
- Forgiving yourself is crucial for breaking free from self-sabotaging victimhood and painful wounds. It leads to true emotional and spiritual healing. SUPERHEROES are NOT VICTIMS!

Set Healthy Boundaries
- Forgiveness doesn't mean accepting abuse or harmful actions. It's essential to set boundaries and distance yourself from toxic influences while maintaining your well-being.

Reclaim Your Authentic Self
- True forgiveness removes energetic cords and attachments, freeing your consciousness. It's a key part of reclaiming your core self and developing spiritual maturity.

Spiritual Maturity
- This journey involves knowing your inner self, balancing your emotions, and achieving inner harmony. It's about going beyond personal dramas and caring for the greater good.

Natural State of Being
- Your natural spiritual state is one of emotional balance, inner peace, and connection with life. This state remains constant, even amidst external chaos.

Self-Control and Responsibility
- Developing self-control and discipline is vital for personal and spiritual growth. It's about balancing your own needs with respect for others, leading to a harmonious life.

Release Attachments
- Let go of attachments with unconditional love and forgiveness. This boosts your spiritual growth and enhances your vibrational energy.
- This is a crucial step to unblocking your lower chakras and ego-self.

Embrace your superhero journey by choosing forgiveness, kindness, compassion, and self-love. Unlock your true power and soar to new heights!

Superhero Mastery: The Power of Neutrality

Stay Neutral and Present
- Healing is non-verbal and non-linear.
- Release your mind from fixating and increase your higher perception.
- Stay fully present in the now.

Key Principles
- No Judgment: Replace it with discernment.
- Fearless and Timeless: Stay in the moment.
- Compassionate Witness: Be a gentle observer.
- Breathe Deeply and Relax: "I am Neutral."

Observer Mode
- Think of it like watching a movie.
- Stay detached, outside the timeline, and recognize that it's just a holographic projection.
- Don't get sucked into the drama; stay outside where it has no power over you.

Politics/News/World Events
- The same applies to observing other timelines. If you get emotionally pulled in, you risk getting hurt.
- Stay detached and maintain your observer status to keep your power.

Skill Set Mastery
- Being neutral doesn't mean you don't care.
- It means you wisely apply your energy and consciousness, focusing on what truly matters.

Embrace the superhero within you by mastering the art of neutrality and observation, empowering yourself to heal and support effectively!

Superhero Forgiveness Meditation

Find a Quiet Space
- Sit comfortably in a peaceful place where you won't be disturbed.

Relax and Center Yourself
- Close your eyes, take a deep breath, and let your body relax. Feel your tension melting away.

Visualize the Past
- Envision everyone who has hurt you in the past. Picture them clearly in your mind's eye.

See Their True Selves
- As you look closer, see them as little children (around age three), using the skills they had at that time. They had no intention to hurt you; they were acting out of their own limitations.

Cut the Cords
- Imagine gently cutting the cords of pain and resentment that tie you to these people. Feel the weight lift off your shoulders.

Choose Love
- Send love and compassion to those children. Embrace them with understanding and kindness.

Transform the Pain
- Watch as they transform into beautiful, illuminated butterflies. See them flutter and fly away, carrying away your pain and anger. **This is how you TRANSMUTE NEGATIVE ENERGY! Remember this!**

Break Free
- As they fly away, feel yourself breaking out of your own cocoon, transforming into the magnificent butterfly you were always meant to be.

Feel Refreshed and Healed
- Breathe deeply and feel a sense of refreshment and healing. Let the forgiveness and compassion fill your heart.

Embrace Your Inner Superhero
- Know that by forgiving, you've tapped into your inner superhero power. Feel the strength and peace within you.

Superhero Insight: ZERO Point & Neutrality

Energetic Balance
- Maintain energetic balance by observing without attachment. This allows divine forces to flow through you, bringing resolution, healing, and peace.

Open the Door to Divinity
- Fear closes the door to divine energies. Inner balance through peace and love opens it wide.

Neutral Observer Mindset
- Adopt a neutral, observer mindset. Remember: OBSERVE, DO NOT ABSORB. Healing doesn't follow a straight path. Let go of mental distractions, focus on intuitive feelings, and stay present.

Compassionate Power
- Compassion, guided by God's essence, is powerful when embodied in a neutral state. It can heal the body, shift timelines, reveal deception, activate the Lightbody, retrieve lost soul fragments, and connect to Universal wisdom.

Unification Tool
- Compassion's core purpose is unification. It resolves, reconciles, and harmonizes. This is the ultimate tool in God's Liquid Light Technology kit.

Compassionate Witness
- Being the Compassionate Witness may be our true purpose, the foundation for a unified humanity. Compassion, free from ego, transforms suffering into powerful awakening for humanity and the planet.

True Love
- True compassionate love creates unity, starting with connecting to our inner being as taught in the Law of One. Embody love to experience God. The journey starts within each of us.
- No judgment, only discernment. Harness the power of compassion and neutrality to unlock your superhero potential and unite humanity!
- Make a choice right now which thoughts you want to own and those you want to discard.
- Set a goal to use the spiritual self-centering model from the **Ascension Light Academy Journal** by Lisa Renee & Chris Mayer. This practice helps you keep your mind balanced and maintain loving and neutral thoughts. Challenge yourself: How long can you stay centered? Track your progress and observe your growth.

We are in the process of dissolving our EGO, it is daily work and acknowledgement
- **Superior Thinking**: Intolerance, Impatience, Arrogance, Manipulation, Attack, Anger, Judgmental thinking.
- **Inferior Thinking**: Worry, Low Self Love or Esteem, Jealousy, Guilt, Hurt, Fear, Attachment, Martrydom.

Behaviors Discernment Guideline

Deception Behavior - Untrustworthy and spiritually abusive behavior	God-Sovereignty Free Behavior - Trustworthy and spiritually healthy behavior
Dissociation and Narcissism	Empathy and Compassion
Mental Rigidity	Mental Openness
Emotional Fracturing	Emotional Stability
Carelessness	Responsibility
Deceitful	Honesty
Dependence	Sovereignty
False Reality Delusions	Reality Assessment
Divided Competition	Unified Cooperation

The key is to always be in the blue on the RIGHT side.

Superhero Shift: Earth's Chakra Evolution

Earth's Chakras (Stargates) - Just like humans, Earth has its own chakra system, known as Stargates. These act to step down higher energies from the Source field into the Sun, which then directs them into various Stargates.
- **Energy Transmission**
    - Stargates transmit an energetic spectrum of frequencies, moving from higher to lower dimensions to reach the matter fields and circulate throughout the planetary grid.
    - They create energy spirals that circulate God Source energy across multiple dimensions, returning to unite with the God Source field.

The Grail Point
- The central Stargate receiving and distributing the Source field energy throughout the planetary grid is known as the Grail Point.

Accelerated Changes
- Just like human chakras are evolving and aligning, Earth's chakras are also undergoing significant changes.
- The transmission of intergalactic plasma waves from the Source field into the Grail Point and Planetary Stargates is greatly accelerating now.

Embrace the superhero shift within and around you, as both human and planetary chakras evolve together, aligning with higher frequencies and unlocking new potentials!

Superhero Evolution: Collapsing Chakra Membranes

Planetary and Chakra Membranes
- As planetary membranes and obsolete dimensional spaces collapse, so do the membranes around the chakra cones.
- This dissolution is part of the Ascension cycle, an evolutionary event.

Readiness for Change
- Some people aren't ready to leave the chakra system yet. They're dependent on energy centers for life force circulation.
- Until they awaken and choose to transcend ego programming, removing these membranes is nearly impossible.

Impact on the Masses - Many are unprepared for these changes, leading to confusion and distress. Currently, all beings on 3D Earth have this configuration in their energy centers.

Spiritual Ascension
- Through spiritual ascension and lightbody development, individuals may evolve past the chakra membranes, integrating their separated identities.

Consciousness Integration
- As consciousness develops, individuals integrate their identities, retrieving and reintegrating missing pieces through the chakra cones.
- This function aligns with the collective consciousness state on Earth.

Pioneers of Light
- Many of us are here to develop our lightbodies and hold the necessary energetic space for the planet and human tribes, becoming prototypes for future generations.
- Our chakras are moving and changing just the Earth's chakras. As we embrace inner healing, we mirror the earth reopening her Stargates.

Superhero Meditation: Healing Your Inner Child

Find a Quiet Space
- Find a peaceful and comfortable place where you won't be disturbed.

Relax and Center Yourself
- Sit or lie down comfortably, close your eyes, and take a few deep breaths. Allow your body to relax and your mind to calm.

Enter Your Heart Space
- Visualize a warm, glowing light in the center of your chest. This is your inner heart space. Feel the warmth and love emanating from this light.

Meet Your Inner Child
- Imagine a doorway in your heart space. As you open the door, you see your inner child – a younger version of yourself. Their face lights up with excitement as they finally meet you

Embrace Your Inner Child
Your inner child runs towards you and jumps into your arms. Hold them close and embrace them with all the love and compassion you have.

Share Words of Love
- Look into your inner child's eyes, and with tears of relief and joy, they say to you, "You're the best part of me."

Send Love and Healing
- Continue to hold your inner child, sending them waves of love, healing, and reassurance. Let them know that they are safe, cherished, and loved.

Integration and Gratitude
- Visualize your inner child merging with your adult self, becoming one. Feel the unity and strength of this integration. Express gratitude for this healing moment.

Return to the Present
- Slowly bring your awareness back to your surroundings. Take a few deep breaths, wiggle your fingers and toes, and gently open your eyes.
- Embrace this healing journey and honor the superhero within you, nurturing your inner child and becoming whole.

Superhero Ascension: Unlocking Cosmic Secrets

Ending Cosmic Cycles
- As we conclude planetary cycles of 26,000 years and galactic cycles of 208,000 years, we're reclaiming lost memories, piecing together a multidimensional puzzle.
- Those journeying along the ascending timeline are experiencing a profound transformation. Their chakra membranes are dissolving, allowing for a deep and holistic healing process. This metamorphosis is not just a physical one, but a spiritual and emotional rejuvenation, leading to a state of harmony and balance. The energy flow within them is becoming more fluid and aligned, paving the way for a higher state of consciousness and well-being.

Alchemical Activations
- Through the Magnum Opus and 13 constellation activations, we progress through Alchemical Laws. The Ophiuchus constellation transmits the powerful Silver-Gold frequency, activating inner Unification.

Fire Water (Ophiuchus, November 30 to December 17)
- A new substance, combining Elemental Water and Aether, emerges through plasmic Silver-Gold light, creating Fire Water, a spiritual element for planetary and human evolution.

Ophiuchus and Orion
- Ophiuchus, the Serpent Holder, aligns with the galactic center, while Orion represents its opposite. Together, they form the ascending path from the Gate of Man to the Gate of the Gods. History removed Ophiuchus from our books and calendars.

Ascension Pathway
- Earthly beings evolve through the Precession of Equinoxes, moving through the Gate of Man and intersecting at Ophiuchus' feet, leading to the Golden Gate. This path guides us to eternal spiritual beings unified with the Cosmic Holy Spirit.

The Gates
- The Golden Gate and Silver Gate mark critical intersection points on the celestial path, representing the union of spiritual masculine and feminine.

Ancient Wisdom
- Ancient Egypt's zodiac includes Ophiuchus and Orion, emphasizing the integration of polarity and spiritual union at the intersection of the gates.

Potential for Healing
- This period offers synchronistic events, energetic resurrection, and healing, accessible through the opening of the Golden Gate.

A Full Disclosure Event refers to the highest level of revealing extraterrestrial information to humans. It would uncover the true hidden Galactic History of humanity, as opposed to the manipulated version used to control mainstream historical records since the Sumerian-Egypt Invasion. Humans would learn not only about the existence of extraterrestrial races, crafts, and agreements with world governments but also about NAA groups, Secret Space Programs, Human Trafficking, Mind Control, Transhumanism, AI agendas, and DNA and genetic manipulation programs both on and off the planet.

Ophiuchus:

Imposter:

Alchemical Theme: Cosmic Trine Unification, Synthesis, Wound Healing

Ophiuchus, the original founder of medicine. Today's global medical system, often corrupted, is symbolized by the rod of Asclepius, a snake-entwined staff.

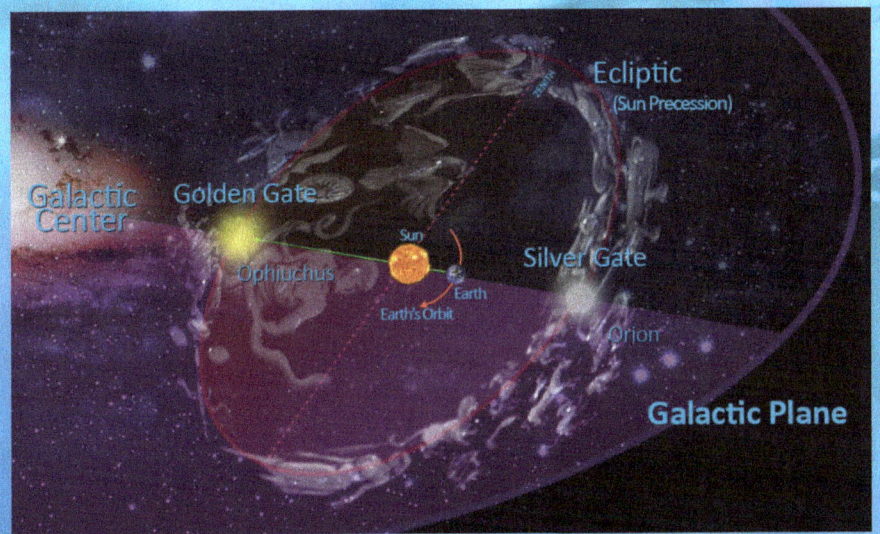

** *Photo from energeticsynthesis.com*

Ophiuchus: The Original Healer
- Ophiuchus, revered for his extraordinary healing abilities, used a magical elixir to bring Orion back to life. This act earned him the title of the founder of medicine, symbolizing true healing and compassion.

Symbol of Healing Corruption
- Today, the global medical system often reflects corruption, symbolized by the rod of Asclepius, a snake-entwined staff. This staff, while a historic symbol of medicine, now represents the tangled complexities and commercial interests overshadowing genuine healthcare.

Return of True Healing
- During the Ophiuchus Solar Alchemy, the authentic spirit of Ophiuchus re-emerges.
- He dispenses universal remedies and magical healing elixirs, gifts from the Solar Goddess Athena, to assist humanity in healing their deepest wounds.

Healing Humanity
- With Ophiuchus' return, the focus shifts back to genuine healing, helping humanity overcome their most profound spiritual and emotional pains, restoring the true essence of medicine.
- Embrace the Galactic Zodiac Imprint and join the journey to authentic wellness and spiritual revival!

Superhero Shift: Earth's Chakra Movements

Earth's chakras, or Stargates, are dynamic and evolving, just like human chakras. Here are some examples of how Earth's chakras are moving and changing:

1. Mount Shasta (Root Chakra)
- Traditionally, Mount Shasta in California is considered Earth's root chakra. It's known for grounding energy.
- Recently, there's been a shift towards more dynamic energy flows, signifying a rise in vibrational frequency.

2. Lake Titicaca (Sacral Chakra)
- Located in Peru and Bolivia, this chakra is linked with creativity and emotion.
- Increased activity here suggests enhanced emotional healing and creative energies.

3. Uluru-Kata Tjuta (Solar Plexus Chakra)
- In Australia, these sacred sites are known for power and will.
- Movement and energy shifts here indicate a strengthening of Earth's core energies, empowering spiritual growth.

4. Glastonbury and Shaftesbury (Heart Chakra)
- In England, this chakra is associated with love and healing.
- There has been a noticeable increase in heart-centered energies, promoting global compassion and unity.

5. Great Pyramid of Giza (Throat Chakra)
- In Egypt, this chakra is about communication and truth.
- Enhanced activity here suggests a global awakening to truth and more open communication.

6. Aeon Activation (Third Eye Chakra)
- This mobile chakra moves according to the spiritual needs of the Earth.
- It's currently seen as activating in locations that enhance intuitive abilities and higher consciousness.

7. Mount Kailash (Crown Chakra)
- In Tibet, this chakra connects to divine consciousness.
- There has been a significant rise in spiritual energies, suggesting an alignment with higher cosmic frequencies.

These shifts show Earth's chakras evolving, aligning with higher energies and frequencies, just like humans on their spiritual journeys.

Have you ever been drawn to any of these areas? If so, you are GRIDWORKER.

Superhero Alert: Planetary Stargates Opening!
- Get ready, superheroes!
- The Planetary Stargate System is Earth's ultimate connection to the Galactic and Universal Stargate Systems.

Planetary Stargates are the Earth's connection points or **Portals** into the Galactic and Universal Stargate Systems. They were once sealed off and closed, but now these Stargates are progressively opening during the Ascension Cycle.

Superhero Mission: Unlocking Universal Consciousness
Opening Portals
- Superheroes, get ready!
- Portals can be opened through higher plasma light, using specialized technology or your own developed inner light and Lightbody.

Earth's Natural Stargates
1D Stargate Sedona, Arizona 35° N, 111.8° W
1D Inner gate Cyprus 35.1264° N, 33.4299° E
2D Stargate Temple Mount 31.7781° N, 35.2360° E
2D Stargate Sarasota, Florida 27.3364° N, 82.5307° W - FPM
2D Inner gate Easter Island, Chile (Grual-Grail Point)
3D Stargate Bermuda Triangle 25° N, 71° W
3D Inner gate Johannesburg, South Africa 26.2041° S, 28.0473° E
4D Stargate Giza, Egypt 29.9753° N 31.1376° E
4D Inner gate Central Mexico, Aguascalientes 21.8853°N, 102.2916° W
5D Stargate Machu Picchu 13.1631° S, 72.545° W
5D Inner Gate Vatican City 41.9029° N, 12.4534° E
6D Stargate Caucasus Mountains at Russia & Georgia border 42.639°N, 44.155°E
6D Inner gate Thar Desert at India & Pakistani border 27.47°N, 70.6°E
7D Stargate Lake Titicaca 15.9254° S, 69.3354° W
7D Inner gate Ionian Islands, city of Gaios on Paxos 39.2°N, 20.18333° E
8D Stargate Xian, China 34.3416° N, 108.9398° E
8D Inner gate Lop Nur, border Tibet/China 40.1666° N, 90.5833° E
9D Stargate Tibet Autonomous Region, Bam Co Lake 31.25277778° N, 90.57861111° E
9D Inner gate Valley of the White Horse, Westbury England 51.26361111° N, 2.14694444°W
10D Stargate Abadan, Iran 30.3°N, 48.3° E
10D Inner gate Basrah, Iraq 30.5081°N, 47.7835° E
11D Stargate Vale of Pewsey, Amesbury, Wiltshire, UK (Stonehenge) 51.1679° N, 1.763° W
11D Inner gate Ireland's Eye, Irish Sea 53.404608° N, 6.063344° W
11D Inner gate St. Ives Bay, Cornwall, UK 50.211° N, 5.48° W (Grual-Grail Point)
12D Stargate Monsegur, southern France 44.65° N, 0.0803° E
12D Inner gate Kauai 22.16444° N, 159.65722° W

Superhero Insight: Galactic Ground Crew

Legions of Light
- The Legions of Light and ground crew are working tirelessly to repair and rehabilitate the timelines and dimensional matrices.

Starseed Heroes
- As members of the Starseed family, we are like human acupuncture points, anchoring galactic frequencies into the planetary grid. Our bodies serve as ascension technology, connecting these energies to specific locations.

Travel to Stargates
- This is why many of us are called to travel to Stargates or vortex locations on the planet. Sometimes, we can do this remotely, while other times we are physically called to be at these points.
- Have you been called to any of these locations? Did you ever wonder **WHY** you were drawn to these places?
- Our presence there helped anchor the necessary frequencies.

As a Starseed hero, embrace your role in the Legions of Light and continue your journey to anchor galactic frequencies, transforming the planet!

Impact of Gamma Rays on Our Consciousness

Our planet is currently immersed in gamma rays—the same powerful waves that transformed Bruce Banner into the Hulk! Were they trying to tell us something? While we may not be turning green and smashing things, these gamma rays are having a profound impact on our brains, bodies, and spiritual development. Let's explore how they tie in with the magical five elements.

Gamma Rays: Supercharged Activation

- **Brain Power**: Gamma rays activate dormant centers in our brain, enhancing cognitive learning and processing. Think of it as unlocking your inner genius without the Hulk-sized temper tantrums.
- **DNA Transformation**: These high-frequency waves stimulate our DNA, aligning it with the purest frequencies of the five elements: fire, aether, air, earth, and water.

The Five Elements - Building Blocks of Magic

- **Elemental Frequencies**: Each element corresponds to a specific color wave: emerald green, azure blue, pale red, golden yellow, and white.
- **Integration**: By aligning with these elemental frequencies, our physical and etheric bodies harmonize, promoting balance and unity.

Spiritual Enlightenment and Cosmic Connections

- **Higher Consciousness**: Gamma rays facilitate profound moments of self-realization and spiritual downloads. Imagine gaining sudden bursts of wisdom and clarity, much like the Hulk figuring out quantum physics.
- **Cellular Telepathy**: These rays enable higher consciousness communication, connecting us with the universe's intelligence and the cosmic energies of the five elements.

Achieving the Rainbow Body

- **Attunement**: Aligning with the gamma rays and elemental frequencies helps reabsorb our DNA's raw materials back into their true spiritual essence, creating organic rainbow consciousness units.
- **Magical Transformation**: This journey leads to the realization of the rainbow body, a state of higher consciousness and spiritual enlightenment.

Rapid Planetary Shifts:
- **Harmonic Resonance**: Cosmic energies entrain our bodies to align with gamma waves, connecting us deeply with the planetary grid.
- **Unity and Interconnection**: Gamma wave oscillations align our minds with the collective consciousness, providing deep insights into the interconnectedness of all life.

So, while gamma rays may have given the Hulk his superpowers, they're giving us an incredible boost in spiritual growth and higher consciousness. Embrace these cosmic waves and the magic of the five elements as they guide you on your journey to becoming your own superhero of enlightenment! If you're struggling with these urges, BREATHE and consider more grounding.

Merging with the Five Elements (Hulk Style!)
When someone completely merges with the five elements, they undergo a dramatic transformation. To an observer, their physical body might shrink drastically or even disappear! But don't worry, they haven't turned into the Hulk—just a higher consciousness form.

Two Types of Rainbow Body in Tibetan Buddhism
Normal Rainbow Body:
- **Death Process**: As the person dies, their consciousness detaches from the physical body. Over a few days, their body shrinks to the size of a toddler or newborn. Some physical remains might be left behind, but the body becomes tiny.

Supreme Transference Rainbow Body:
- **Full Conscious Exit**: Here, the entire body and consciousness are absorbed into the natural elements. No death involved! The body simply vanishes, leaving behind flashes of white light and rainbows (no green smashing involved).

Spiritual Requirements:
- **Pure Hearts:** This rare supreme transference requires a pure crystal heart filled with love.
- **Service to Others:** Achieving these states means dedicating oneself to virtue, ethics, and helping others. The Sun doesn't charge you for SOLAR POWERING your body, so why do energy workers? [Refer to the Law of One Section, pages 86-89]. The Law of One has been distorted and twisted to justify self-gain at the Collective's expense.

Beware the Ego Trap
Responsibility
- Spiritual knowledge needs responsibility.
- Chasing supernatural powers for personal gain is risky and can lead to negative consequences.

Ascension and Ego Death
- The Guardians have a cosmic update: during the Ascension Cycle, those on the ascension path might experience a "death-like" transition.
- This phenomenon occurs when life experiences flash before our eyes, allowing us to become aware of the emotions tied to memories from the past, present, and future. It is linked to the death process, where the soul matrix releases gamma wave frequencies into the brain to separate the physical body from the consciousness layers.

What to Expect
- **Ego Death**: You might feel like you've been through this ego death in past lives.
- **Deceased Loved Ones**: You may see deceased loved ones or perceive your own death and rebirth cycles.
- **Consciousness Growth**: Don't worry, you're not actually dropping your physical body. You're just leveling up your consciousness to integrate all parts of your identity into your ascending self.

Gamma Ray Sensations
- **Surreal Disorientation**: The rapid increase of gamma rays might make you feel like your soul is leaving your body, or you might experience some bizarre physical sensations.
- **Spiritual Phenomena**: These gamma rays can trigger major shifts in consciousness, leading to some pretty wild spiritual phenomena.
- Additionally, cosmic energy from the galactic center is sending gamma waves through the Sun Disc network of various constellations.
- These waves are unifying the hemispheres of the human brain and shifting consciousness.
- This unification is causing deeper harmonic resonance shifts, which may trigger sudden and spontaneous gamma wave oscillations in the brain, leading to sequences of higher consciousness events.

Gamma Waves and Cosmic Protection
- When gamma wave oscillations hit our brains, it's like the Hulk's own protective armor—but for our bio-neurology!

Here's the scoop:

Cosmic Shield
- **Gamma Waves**: These waves bring in the Cosmic Mother's protective plasmic sheath, a bit like a magical, glowing bubble wrap for your brain and nervous system.

Meditation Boost: Practicing meditation increases these gamma waves, strengthening this protective layer.

Heart-Centered Lifestyle
- **Compassionate Living**: Leading a heart-centered, compassionate lifestyle supercharges these protective gamma waves.
- **Energy Shield**: These waves protect our bio-neurology from harmful frequencies and mind control signals, like AI signals trying to mess with us.

In short, gamma waves are your brain's superhero armor, ready to protect and defend against any unwanted invaders. Just think of it as Hulk's strength combined with the cosmic power of meditation and a compassionate heart!

The SpaceWeatherLive App: Just like Hulk's transformation, this app is your FREE go-to for monitoring space weather and incoming gamma rays. Here's *why I love it* -

- **Monitor Space Weather:**
  - **Solar Activity**: Keep an eye on solar flares and other space phenomena, just like Bruce Banner would keep track of his own gamma levels.
  - **Auroras and Geomagnetic Storms**: See the stunning effects of these cosmic events, no Hulk-sized rage needed!

- **User-Friendly Features:**
  - **Beginner-Friendly**: Easy to navigate, even if you're new to space weather.
  - **Dark Mode**: Perfect for those late-night gamma-ray checks, keeping your vision sharp just like Banner's intellect.

- **Stay Alert:**
  - **Push Notifications**: Get instant updates on significant space events. It's like having a gamma-powered alarm system!

- **Auoras/Northern Lights**: Granted, I can never stay awake late enough to witness them, but it's on this FREE APP as well.

Different SOLAR FLASH Classifications

α – Alpha:	A unipolar sunspot group.
β – Beta:	A sunspot group that has a positive and a negative polarity (or bipolar) with a simple division between the polarities.
γ – Gamma:	A complex region in which the positive and negative polarities are so irregularly distributed that they can't be classified as a bipolar Sunspot group.
β-γ – Beta-Gamma:	A bipolar sunspot group but complex enough so that no line can be drawn between spots of opposite polarity.
δ – Delta:	The umbrae of opposite polarity in a single penumbra.
β-δ – Beta-Delta:	A sunspot group with a general beta magnetic configuration but contains one (or more) delta sunspots.
β-γ-δ – Beta-Gamma-Delta:	A sunspot group with a beta-gamma magnetic configuration but contains one (or more) delta sunspots.
γ-δ – Gamma-Delta:	A sunspot group with a gamma magnetic configuration but contains one (or more) delta sunspots.

More than half of the observed sunspot groups receive an Alpha or Beta classification, where bigger sunspots are often more complex and get a Beta, Beta-Gamma or Beta-Gamma-Delta classification. It is well known that delta sunspots can be very active and produce the most intense solar flares.

The Delta Classification - Let's dig a bit deeper into the magnetic delta class. This is the most interesting type of sunspot structure due to the high solar activity which they often cause. With the following list you can determine whether a sunspot has a magnetic delta structure:

1. Delta groups are often very big and 90 percent of the sunspots have a reversed polarity with a high activity level, especially when big solar flares erupt. These have mostly a complex, unusual or broken view of the umbra.

2. Delta groups are formed by the aggregation of sunspots with opposite polarity of various dipoles, which are linked to shared magnetic field lines rather than direct magnetic lines. All spots are located in the penumbral region.

3. Delta spots rarely last longer than one rotation of the Sun. They decay quicker then other sun spots. However, new delta spots can form within the same area.

4. Delta sunspot groups usually do not separate, but rather die together.

5. Active delta groups emit strong H-alpha emissions. Sometimes filaments can come out of the group.

GRIDWORKERS

Superhero Insight: Planetary Gridworkers on a Mission

Galactic Gridworkers
- Gridworkers have a variety of important tasks and jobs that are tied to the current planetary crisis or issues impacting Earth's body and collective consciousness.
- Our mission spans past, present, and future timelines to create positive changes for humanity's evolution.

Personal Missions
- Each of us has a unique mission based on our special talents and skills. These skills connect us to the larger Starseed and Indigo mission.
- Many Gridworkers come from future cycles of other star systems, universes, and planets to help Earth and humanity ascend and liberate from negative forces.

Challenges
- Starseeds often face challenges like psychotronic mind control, psychic attacks, and dark interference.
- Our mission with Earth is co-created in pre-birth agreements and written into our Lightbody.

Activating Potential
- To activate Starseed potential, we are led to the Law of One, 12D Ray, Alien Implant removal, and studying the 12 Tree Grid.
- This helps awaken our spiritual consciousness and activate higher potentials.

Gridworker Tasks
- **Energy Conduit:** Acting as a conduit for higher frequency transmissions, aligning and correcting planetary grid networks.
- **Timelines:** Traveling or remote viewing to observe and correct historical records, measure energetic impacts, and track causality of events.
- **Recode EMF Rays:** Surveying and recoding energetic currents to elevate into tri-wave code, improving planetary grid networks.
- **Geomantic Structures:** Reconnecting structures, opening portals, activating power vortices, and clearing black magic grids.
- **Inspection and Repair:** Inspecting and repairing damaged planetary grid networks, alien machinery, and artificial intelligence technology.
- **False Records:** Identifying, removing, and repairing false records and clearing destructive events.

- **Transit Services:** Providing transit services for stuck or confused souls and reading rights for negative entities.
- **Join the Mission:** Even if you're not a Gridworker, you may feel the effects of the planetary shifts. We all act as acupuncture points for ascending Earth.
- **Inner Knowing:** If you are a Starseed or Gridworker, you have an inner knowing of these changes. Those without the frequency activation level won't feel anything except observing planetary climatic changes. It's important to remember this as you observe your surroundings. Many people around you may seem completely unaware of these shifts. This is due to their frequency accretion level and DNA capacity.

Superhero Insight: Navigating Harmonic Universes

Gateway to Higher Dimensions
- In the structure of Harmonic Universes, each dimensional octave contains two timelines.
- In our 3D Earth, we have six timelines within the three dimensions. As we evolve energetically and ascend to higher frequencies, we unlock access to more dimensional octaves and additional timelines.

Reclaiming Our Spiritual Identity
- Within these future timelines are stations of identity known as soul, oversoul, and higher self.
- Our mission is to reclaim these spiritual identities during the timeline collapses of the Ascension cycle.

Healing and Growth
- On the ascension path, we continually experience energetic healing by revisiting cellular memories in multiple timelines.
- We must move through these timelines to reclaim our identity, while recoding and transforming obsolete realities.
- Like superheroes leaping over hurdles, we merge with these time fields to collect our spiritual bodies and reach the finish line.

Guardian Ascension Timeline
- To arrive at the GOD GATEWAY, we must navigate through artificial, inorganic time fields and negative alien timelines.
- These false timelines were designed to deter humanity from natural ascension.
- We must overcome these challenges to achieve our divine destiny.

Speeding Up Evolution
- The original 5D plan required rapid evolution through time fields in Harmonic Universes. Those serving the Law of One are moving through vast future timelines, observing their collapse, to reach the Gateway Octave where organic light overrides artificial coding.

Reclaiming Divinity
- By reclaiming our spiritual identity, we rediscover our true divinity as sovereign beings connected to God Source. This leads us to safety and freedom through the maze of confusion. Moving through dimensional octaves is like moving forward in time, aligning us with higher frequencies and future time fields.

Different Levels of Evolution
- People on 3D Earth are at different levels of spiritual evolution. Their frequency and stability determine their future direction, regardless of their awareness. Those who advanced into their soul bodies (4D-5D-6D) enter the next Harmonic Universe, experiencing six more potential timelines.

Joining the Mission
- Even if you're not a Gridworker, you may feel the effects of planetary shifts. Take care of your body and know you're not alone in this process.

Superhero Insight: Ascending to the Oversoul Harmonic Universe

Unlocking Higher Dimensions
- When a person advances into their oversoul or monad bodies (7D-8D-9D), they enter the frequency of the next Harmonic Universe.
- This transition exposes them to another six potential timelines.

Activating Cellular Memories
- These timelines activate cellular memory clearing, allowing the individual to remember and reclaim their identities within those timelines.
- This process is a direct pathway of spiritual ascension, helping beings re-integrate all parts of themselves.

Journey of Re-Integration
- The oversoul Harmonic Universe, parallel to 7D Earth, offers the next six potential timelines.
- Beings working in 7D, known as the Ascended Masters, focus on their divine agenda within these timelines.

Superhero Insight: Guardians of Plasma Light

Raising Earth's Frequencies
- The Guardians of Krystal Star consciousness are streaming plasma waves into Earth's blueprint to raise her frequencies and anchor plasma infusions from Galactic Solar Light.
- They've acquired solar plasma light from the Suns of Sirius B, transmitting Aqualine Healing Energy into Earth.

Plasma Light Transmission
- This allows us to receive and transmit plasma light directly from Earth. Previously, Starseed gridworkers had to go off-planet to gather these frequencies.
- Now, we can connect with Galactic Sun frequencies right from Earth.

Activating Inner Sun Frequencies
- Plasma infusions weave Solar light from Galactic Suns into Earth's core, activating Mother Earth's Inner Sun frequencies.
- These appear as deep ultraviolet and bluish plasma light.
- The blue flame (from 5D core) and violet flame (from 7D core) unite with Galactic Sun counterparts, creating a complete circuit called Aqualine Sun frequencies.

Natural Conduits
- Mother Earth's frequencies merge from deep inside the core through Galactic layers, uniting with Galactic Suns. Indigos, Starseeds, and the Oraphim are the first waves transmitting Aqualine Sun frequencies into Earth, anchoring plasma infusions and repairing networks.

Superhero Insight: Crystal Caverns and Planetary Power

Crystal Caverns' Historical Power
- In planetary history, Crystal Caverns were used as power generators and data storage for the planetary brain.
- These crystals, remnants of the Atlántian era, caused a massive surface cataclysm when misused and now form part of the Reversal NET (electronic force field) running alien frequencies through Earth's crust.
- These <u>NETs</u> are Black Hole Technologies that were created in <u>Atlantian Cataclysm</u> to keep Earth and her life forms in a prison planet.
- The NET fields keep the DNA block locked in. Why haven't humans evolved?

Ancient Earth Shielding - Cosmic Interference
- Around 25,500 BC, powerful scalar sonic pulses were used on Earth's inner grid system, creating an electrostatic force-field known as the NET.

Signal Quarantine
- This NET acts as a barrier, blocking incoming and outgoing signals to higher dimensions and creating a kind of quarantine.
- The NET blankets civilization, cutting off natural connections to inner consciousness and spiritual levels. It interfaces with human existence, creating a Holographic Insert.

Selenite Rods as Data Chips
- Selenite Rods (Gypsum) act like giant computer chips, storing immense planetary data.
- They transmit this information to the planetary brain and the human collective Soul Matrix, affecting all life on Earth.

Unconscious Mind of the Planet
- These crystals send electromagnetic impulses to the planetary field, functioning like the planet's unconscious mind.
- The Sirian A's, famous for crystal programming, sometimes abused this for mind control.

Crystals as Data Keys
- These crystals are keys to the planetary data program and have been held hostage since their explosion thousands of years ago, containing secrets of alien civilizations and Earth's hidden histories.

Superhero Insight: Crystalline Powers and Planetary Harmony

Focus and Energy
- Struggling with attention deficit, obsessions, or anxiety can drain our energy and focus, making it tough to raise consciousness.

Crystal Caverns' Importance
- The Crystal Caverns on our planet play a crucial role.
- These majestic caverns help us understand how bio-plasma transforms into matter and show that the higher substance of the cosmos, Plasma, is present in crystals.

Crystalline Forms and Consciousness
- As we expand our consciousness during the Ascension Cycle, we connect more with crystalline properties.
- This relationship directly impacts the planetary brain, which affects our individual brain functions.

Healthy Brain Chemistry
- Quartz crystals are linked to amygdala functions, influencing our limbic system. A well-functioning planetary brain means healthier brain chemistry and balanced neurological impulses for us.

Gridworkers and Planetary Brain
- Gridworkers, working on the planet's grid, are essentially enhancing the planet's neurological system and brain.
- This work impacts us at the micro level, as we are all nerve cells and extensions of this neural network.

Crystal Shelves or Crystal Caverns
Central Oregon
Arkansas
Sequoia National Park, CA
Mt. Shasta, CA
Florida Coastal Sands
Bimini Islands
British Columbia, Canada
Ontario, Canada
Naica, Central Mexico
Brasila, Minas Gerais, Brazil
Namibia, Africa
Grimsel, Switzerland
Belize
Giza, Egypt
Lake Titicaca, Bolivia side
Siberia, Russia
Scotland
Sri Lanka
Xian, China
Uluru, Australia

Superhero Insight: Crystalline Pathways

Geologic Shelves of Crystals
- Massive geologic shelves stretch from Naica in Chihuahua, Mexico, through Central Mexico, to Guatemala. These shelves hold gigantic crystals like Selenite, Fluorite, and other quartz crystals.

Crystal Cavern in Naica
- The Crystal Cavern in Naica is a Parallel Gate, a wormhole to a Parallel Universe.
- Inner Gate at Aguascalientes
- About 550 miles south of Naica, the Inner Gate at Aguascalientes leads underground to the Giza/Sphinx. This area also contains massive underground shelves of crystals.

EMERALD TABLETS

Superhero Insight: Cloister Dora Teura (CDT) and the Emerald Covenant

Cloister Dora Teura (CDT)
- Refers to 12 holographic disc records made of selenite quartz crystals, created in Sirius B.
- Contain the evolutionary history of life throughout the Universal Time Matrix.
- Sourced from the great Cosmic Hall of Records as the Maharata Teachings of the Universal Melchizedek Lineages of the Cosmic Christos.

Founder Records and Emerald Covenant
- Also known as the Emerald Covenant CDT Holographic Plates.
- Originally belonged to the Human 12 Tribes and contained principal spiritual teachings during the Lemurian and early Atlantean timelines.
- Each disc was protected by an assigned Maji Grail King, the main Guardian of the planetary stargate of his tribe.

Emerald Covenant Teachings
- Contained knowledge about the origins, genetics, and purpose of the human race.
- Included historical timeline accounts of Galactic history, the divine birthright of all angelic humans.
- Described the consciousness mechanics of reality, manifestation, and unification with the eternal, loving, One God Source.
- Taught humans to activate their light body through consciousness training for full liberation as a Cosmic Christos.
- Protected by Founder Guardians in an ancient genetic library until more humans could awaken.

Protection and Preservation
- Sirian High Council members, primarily from the Universal Christos lineages, guarded and preserved these sacred records.
- Archivists mapped out the DNA code as the genetic library for all creations throughout the 12 organic timelines.

Advanced Technological Information
- The discs contained information on planetary templar stargates, Ley Lines, and the Law of One teachings.
- Unified sacred sciences with spirituality.
- *I hope this book will return this information and knowledge to you*

Superhero Insight: Stolen Founder Records

Thoth's Betrayal
- Approximately 22,000 years ago, Thoth led a militarized event resulting in the Essene Massacre.
- Males were murdered, and their sacred marriage female partners were taken hostage for forced hybridization breeding on Nibiru.

Theft of Sacred Knowledge
- Thoth stole the CDT plate in their possession. From this stolen knowledge, he wrote down information that later became the basis of Hermeticism and the Emerald Tablet.

Impact on Human Evolution
- This event triggered a significant change in human evolution, forming controlled beliefs and Luciferian elitism around Hermeticism, esoteric Kabbalah, Mystery Schools, and Secret Societies.

Hidden Knowledge
- These secret societies, originally formed by the Luciferian Knights Templar, were designed to hide ancient sacred knowledge of humanity's true origins from the common people, directing them into superstitions, ignorance, and organized religion.

Superhero Insight: 12 Essene Tribes

12 Essene Tribes
- The Emerald Founder Records reveal the 12 Essene Tribes form the entirety of the human gene pool, descending from the Universal Tribal Shield.
- They originally incarnated on this planet from future timelines of Tara.

Genetic Key Codes
- Each tribe is genetically key coded to their Planetary Gates location, the planetary dimensional sphere, and its ley line network. Our DNA contains genetic time codes related to this system, part of our Human Tribal Identity.

Activation of Inner Christos
- We activate our human tribal identity and personal planetary keys by running the 12D Ray, creating 144 harmonics throughout our Lightbody (the 12D Shield).
- This identity has had many lifetimes participating in consciousness evolution and assembling DNA codes in the angelic human Root Races throughout the Solar System.

Evolution Plan
- The original 12 Essene Tribes were seeded on Earth as part of the Covenant of Paliador's evolution plan.
- This was to rescue lost Souls of Tara and reclaim these identities when the stargates opened at the end of the Ascension Cycle.

Platonic Solids

Core Patterns of Creation

The Mystery Schools of Pythagoras, Plato, and the ancient Greeks taught that five Platonic Solids are the core patterns behind physical creation:
- Earth
- Fire
- Air
- Water
- Aether (Universal Substance)

Dodecahedron's Power
- The dodecahedron, representing Aether, was closely guarded due to its potential misuse.
- Through Hieros Gamos, the dodecahedron is upgraded to the Star of Azoth, connecting to the Krystal Star Seven Sacred Suns, governed by Cosmic Sovereign Law.

Cosmic Aether
- Cosmic Aether, or Mother's Quintessence, manifests into geometrical wave patterns, creating fractal patterns of matter.
- Platonic Solids arrange in fractal patterns, forming a Morphogenetic Field and a matrix in space, interconnecting atoms with celestial patterns.

Universal Movements
- Following the Hermetic principle "As Above, So Below," these celestial patterns are part of the Sun's elliptical path through constellations, moving through evolutionary cycles called the Precession of the Equinoxes.
  - The phrase itself is a popular modern paraphrase of the second verse of the Emerald Tablet, an ancient text attributed to Hermes Trismegistus.
- The Universe evolves through spirals, with a central core called the eye, representing absolute zero or calm center in consciousness.

Characteristics of Platonic Solids:
- All faces are the same size.
- All edges are the same length.
- Only one angle throughout the entire shape.
- All points touch the edge of a sphere perfectly.
- Platonic Solids as Sonic Geometry.

Earth and Platonic Solids

Sonic geometries, Light Symbol Codes, are based on Platonic solid shapes. These are directed as light programs into one dimension, sending appropriate sound frequencies into the dimension above. Sound makes geometric forms visible through light, intertwining male and female principles in creation.

Platonic Solids as Sonic Geometry

Earth and Platonic Solids
- Sonic geometries, Light Symbol Codes, are based on Platonic solid shapes.
- These are directed as light programs into one dimension, sending appropriate sound frequencies into the dimension above.
- Sound makes geometric forms visible through light, intertwining male and female principles in creation.

Tetrahedron
- Triangle with four sides.
- Represents the element of fire.
- Related to Jupiter and Mars.

Hexahedron
- Square with six faces.
- Represents the element of earth.
- Related to Saturn and Jupiter.

Octahedron
- Triangle with eight faces.
- Represents the element of air.
- Related to Mars and Earth.

Dodecahedron
- Pentagon with twelve faces.
- Represents time and space substance.
- Related to Earth and Venus.

Icosahedron
- Triangle with twenty faces.
- Represents the element of water.
- Related to Venus and Mercury.

Superhero Insight: The Sun as a Stargate

Solar Portal
- Our local star, Sol, is more than just a Sun—it's a Stargate!
- Certain craft can travel in and out of the Solar System via this Solar portal, making it a vital and contested outpost.
- The 4th-dimensional Stargate on Earth is located in Giza, Egypt, opening into the Astral Plane.
- This pathway connects the Sun and Earth through geometric fields based on Platonic Solids, the building blocks of the Universe.
- Anunnaki Control - Thousands of years ago, the Anunnaki took control of this area to dominate the Sun's relationship with Earth and its plasma energy.
- The Sun's activity is crucial for activating human DNA and controlling access to the Solar portal.

Cosmic Web
- Each Sun and Star in the Universe are interconnected through Morphogenetic Fields and plasma filaments, creating a web that links all star consciousness together.

Ascension Cycle
- During the Ascension Cycle, Solar Flares and Stellar Activations dissolve dimensional frequency barriers, merging consciousness energy with biological life forms and shifting them through dimensional time cycles.

Eighth Star of Seven Sisters
- Our Solar System is realigning with the Pleiades (Seven Sisters) star cluster.
- This magnetic synchronization purges collective human miasma and nullifies trauma timelines.
- Solar plasma streams entering the magnetosphere activate the Crystal Body with new DNA tones, aligning humanity with the solar codes of the Seven Sisters DNA.

Solar Streams from the Pleiades
- The return of Solar Christ Michael and Solar Christ Mary brings golden cube solar codes, activating the human Crystal Body and DNA. These streams are building the krystal holographic architecture for an upcoming density shift, radically changing Earth's and the Sun's magnetism.

Momentous Solar System Shift
- The Solar System's eleven main celestial bodies are synchronizing with the shifting magnetic core of our Sun. As the eighth Sun Star from the Pleiades (Seven Sisters), our Sun's magnetic core realigns with these stars during mid-May to mid-June, purging collective human trauma from the Fall of Tara.

Solar Winds and Magnetic Reconfiguration
- Solar winds entering the magnetosphere control Earth's magnetic field, now reconfiguring into organic magnetism.
- This dismantles artificial constructs and mind control programming, dissolving 3D consciousness layers and causing ego death spiritual crises for some.

Tri-Wave Solar Plasma
- The acceleration of tri-wave solar plasma light currents is inspiring matter through solar symbiosis, blending physical matter with solar fire plasma light symbol codes.
- This rearranges Crystal Body templates and impacts human DNA instruction sets.

New Magnetic Wave Pattern
- Solar plasma streams entering the magnetosphere create a new magnetic wave resonance in Earth's grid, amplifying Crystal Body activation with new DNA tones.
- This ascension wave attunes the human light body with the solar codes of the Seven Sisters DNA, supporting humanity through planetary ascension and future disclosure events.

Superhero Insight: Magnetic Sound Tone Upgrades

Emerald Ray Activation
- The new magnetic wave tone in the crystal core, known as the Cosmic Monad or Emerald Ray, is shifting the outer grids' density and retuning their magnetic sound tones.

Electromagnetic Synchronization
- This rapid density shift requires synchronization between inner and outer domains, connecting with Emerald Ray sound tones that create new elemental forces and alter the magnetosphere.

Electromagnetic Synchronization
- This rapid density shift requires synchronization between inner and outer domains, connecting with Emerald Ray sound tones that create new elemental forces and alter the magnetosphere.

Magnetic Shifts and Spin Rate
- Sound elementals produce magnetic shifts, changing the rotational spin of energy fields in the planetary grid. This activates atoms to adjust their spin rate in our cells, increasing frequency and vibration.

Geomagnetic Shifts and Wobbles
- Geomagnetic shifts cause wobbles, interrupting Earth's spin and affecting the light spectrum we see, brain functions, and our neural-spiritual interface. Symptoms may include temporary loss of motor skills, blurry vision, dizziness, and more.

Angelic Human DNA Changes
- Magnetic shifts in the iron core and magnetosphere influence the human DNA template, causing physical upgrades and intense ascension symptoms.
- These shifts impact brain functions and biological rhythms, leading to possible disorienting experiences like a "glitch in the matrix" effect.
- No, you're not broke!!

Magnetic Biological Reset
- This reset can cause temporary glitches in peripheral body parts, large joints, or limbs, with short-term loss of function.

Rapid Transformation
- The bifurcating population is undergoing rapid transformation through Crystal Body activation. This process helps the higher monadic spiritual identity decide the best direction for spiritual progress.

Evolutionary Crossroads
We're at a crucial evolutionary marker, facing intense consciousness transformation. Not everyone will be prepared to handle this shift.

Spiritual Decisions
The higher consciousness monadic identity must choose to either:
- Walk through painful disclosure events and global awakening to spiritually integrate back into wholeness.
- Leave this realm and move to an ascension-hosted plane with integrated consciousness support in a spiritual trauma healing environment.

Unstoppable Liberation
- The planet's liberation is inevitable. Those who resist or obstruct the collective consciousness evolution through planetary ascension and disclosure will either leave voluntarily or be removed as they deteriorate.

Superhero Insight: Light Symbol Codes and DNA Signal
Energetic Exchanges
- Living our highest spiritual expression exposes us to higher frequencies and light symbol codes from our monad, Avatar Christos, and higher spiritual identities. These codes activate the Crystal Body, directing consciousness energy and arranging new musical DNA tones.

DNA Musical Tones
- New DNA musical tones activate higher DNA potentials, adjusting the physical body.
- These tones organize the raw material of DNA, like nucleotides and protein chains.
- Human red blood cells emit DNA signals, so it's crucial to avoid injecting foreign DNA into our bloodstream, which blocks human DNA communication.

Mind Control and Light Codes
- Controllers use light symbol codes in mind control to prevent Crystal Body activation, keeping human DNA dormant. Light codes can program the body for health or, with negative intent, cause fear, disease, and deterioration.

DNA Alignment and Ascension
- Perfect alignment of our DNA signal with Earth's harmonic phasing allows access to species memory and ascension codes.
- Misalignment from hybridization requires bioregenesis and spiritual rehabilitation, leading to the recognition of the Christ Consciousness DNA Signal.

Harness the power of the Solar Stargate to unlock your superhero potential and navigate cosmic transformations! The SUN IS TRANSFERRING SOLAR RAYS TO ACTIVATE YOUR DNA!!

Superhero Insight: Planetary Ascension

Transformation for All
- Every living being on Earth will experience a transformation, resulting in a consciousness shift and ascension event, regardless of their belief system.

Elevating Consciousness
- Those who refuse to move beyond negative ego and awaken their heart center to practice unity, unconditional love, peace, and compassion will leave the planet.

Choices and Ascension
- Although everyone will experience the ascension event, not all will choose to remain on Earth and ascend. Those who don't will return to the spiritual world or a Guardian-hosted interdimensional transit station for reeducation beyond mind control.

Mass Consciousness Transition
- This process, known as the "load out stage" through the Trinity Gates, has already begun and will continue, transiting souls during the bifurcation of time.

Navigating the Bifurcation Load Out

Emotional Challenges
- Observing the bifurcation load out stage during global events can be emotionally tough, especially for those unaware of the painful truths and revelations. It's crucial to stay strong and prepare.

Lightworkers and Starseeds
- This is a time to use your spiritual tools, stay flexible and adaptable, and maintain a calm, peaceful observer consciousness. Be ready to face spontaneous changes in perception.

Human Liberation
- This is a momentous time for human liberation. Pray, meditate, and awaken to the emotional betrayals being revealed. Understand the significance of these events.

Radical Self-Care
- Practice radical self-care and know your physical and emotional limits. Support your loved ones and friends as best as you can during these transformative times.

Simplified Insight: Earth's Crystal Core Shifting

Aspect	Details
Crystal Core Shifting	Changes in Earth's Crystal Core affect matter, atmosphere, and pressure, impacting blood pressure and heart rhythm.
Impact on Matter	Crystal Core influences magnetic field, temperature, composition, and perception of reality.
Morphogenesis	Activation shifts Crystal Core structure, changing matter to new states, making solids less dense.
Crystalline Grid Activation	New instructions release crystalline current, activating Sun Discs and Sun-Star crystals.
Kundalini Recoding	Corrected patterns rebuild mental body and support higher consciousness integration.
Plasma Infusions	Infusions from Galactic Suns increase pearlescent waves, supporting planetary ascension.
Seven Sacred Suns	Unite to transmit Cosmic Sun-Star waves, building Christos Diamond Sun body.
Impact on Time Perception	Crystal Core changes affect matter and anti-matter, impacting perception of time.
New Base Shield Template	Replaces 3D grounding mechanism, building Eukachristic Body and Krystallah eternal lightbody.

Simplified Insight: Crystal Properties

Aspect	Details
Crystal Structure	Crystals are solid structures with atoms arranged in a lattice. Common elements in crystals originate from Earth's crust and have unique properties like color and frequency.
Silicate Crystals	Most Earth's rocks are silicate minerals, forming basic crystal structures in the planet and human body.
Advanced Technologies	Silicate crystals used in technologies reveal similarities with human crystalline consciousness. Silicon, a semiconductor, powers electronic circuits.
Electromagnetic Charge	Crystals must balance negative and positive charges to create energetic balance. Human bodies, like crystals, return to balance by following natural laws.
Crystals as Records	Crystals hold living consciousness records and amplify light frequencies, used for communication, energy production, and data storage.
Historical Significance	Ancient cultures knew crystals controlled energy grids and supported spiritual connection.
Unique Properties	Crystals have unique energetic signatures, impacting energy, frequency, and vibration.
Human Body Crystalline Properties	Human and Earth bodies are made of crystalline properties. The Silicate Matrix DNA template is activated by hydroplasmic light. Bone structure acts as the main frequency transducer.
Energetic Balance	Maintaining life force flow through physical structures is key to health. Humans can amplify, absorb, store, and transmit vibrational energies.

Superhero Cosmic Update: October 2023 Shift

Separation of Worlds
- In October 2023, 3D Lunar Matrix split from the new 5D Sun-Star Networks. This means - between the Lunar Calendar distortions of the 3D zodiacal calendar positions and another new formation with corrected Sun-Star Networks aligning the 5D zodiacal calendar positions. The corrected Solar Calendar positions for the ascending timeline zodiacal alignments have now begun.

Solar Calendar Anchored
- Higher timeline Solar Calendar positions are anchored, there is no turning back. & Return of the Ascended Masters.

Blueprint Barrier
- Solar positions create a barrier between 3D and 5D timelines.
- Consciousness Shifts.
- Expect intense solar activations and purging of old energies.
- This means that the magnetic imprint received from the zodiac constellation alignments at birth will cease to have the same influence upon our body, our personality, our mind and this will impact many other factors.
- From the Guardian perspective, the Galactic Zodiac includes another important constellation called Ophiuchus, which is the missing 13th constellation that acts as the unifier and trine force for all of the other twelve constellations during the Ascension Cycle.

Superhero Insight: Cosmic Ascension and Reactions

Cosmic Elohei Pathway
- If you're on the ascension pathway of the Cosmic Elohei family, your presence can *cause strong reactions in others.* You will sense an unspoken clash.

Lunar vs. Solar Imprints
- Those with lunar zodiac birth imprints may struggle with the major consciousness shifts when encountering someone with newly activated Solar Zodiac Imprints.

Superhero Zodiac: 13 Sign Adventure

Celestial Plane
- Alchemical principles are activated through star constellations. Dr. Percy Seymour and Vasilis Kanatas introduced a new, accurate astrological theory based on the time the Sun spends in each constellation.
- The movement of celestial bodies affects the solar magnetic field, influencing Earth's geomagnetic field and impacting electromagnetic, chemical, and biological systems.

Please only take what resonates with you and discard the rest. I will be disclosing some information that coined the phrase "conspiracy theorist" and that's okay.

13 Sign Zodiac

- The 13 sign zodiac informs of the alchemical principles activated during the phases the Sun spends in the constellations.
- Dates may slightly vary each year for accuracy.
- The 13th Constellation Connects to the Galactic Center: Ophiuchus aligns with the Cosmic Aether at the core of the Galactic Center, symbolizing the pouring of healing spiritual waters into Earth and humanity.

Sign	Dates	Alchemical Theme	Element
Aries	Apr 19 - May 13	Purification, Calcination	Fire
Taurus	May 14 - Jun 19	Congelation, Transformation	Earth
Gemini	Jun 20 - Jul 20	Fixation, Synthesis	Air
Cancer	Jul 21 - Aug 9	Dissolution, Dismantling	Water
Leo	Aug 10 - Sep 15	Digestion, Conversion	Fire
Virgo	Sep 16 - Oct 30	Distillation, Purity	Earth
Libra	Oct 31 - Nov 22	Sublimation, Transmutation	Air
Scorpio	Nov 23 - Nov 29	Separation, Stillness	Water
Ophiuchus	Nov 30 - Dec 17	Unification, Wound Healing	Water/Aether
Sagittarius	Dec 18 - Jan 18	Incineration, Resurrection	Fire
Capricorn	Jan 19 - Feb 15	Fermentation, Illumination	Earth
Aquarius	Feb 16 - Mar 11	Multiplication, Virtues	Air
Pisces	Mar 12 - Apr 18	Ascension, Perfection, Christos-Sophia	Water/Aether

What is your new Galactic Zodiac Imprint? This is your new birth - location. Log your new Galactic Zodiac in your Journal if you keep one.

Physiology Correlated to Galactic Zodiac

- Aries - brain, cerebral hemispheres, cranium, eyes, face, upper jaw, internal carotid arteries, thalamus, adrenals.
- Taurus - neck, throat, palate, larynx, tonsils, lower jaw, ears, occipital region, cerebellum, atlas, axis, external carotid arteries, jugular veins, pharynx, thyroid gland, cervical vertebrae.
- Gemini - shoulders, arms, hands, upper ribs, lungs, trachea, bronchi, capillaries, breath, oxygenation of blood.
- Cancer - stomach, esophagus, diaphragm, breasts, nipples, lacteals, upper lobes of liver, thoracic duct, pancreas, serum of blood, peristalsis of the stomach, gastric fluids, pituitary.
- Leo - heart, dorsal region of spine, spinal cord, aorta, superior and inferior vena cava, thymus.
- Virgo - abdominal region, large and small intestines, lower lobe of liver, spleen, duodenum, thymus secretions, peristalsis of the bowels, pancreas.
- Libra - kidneys, adrenals, lumbar region, skin, ureters, vasomotor system, medulla, ovaries.
- Scorpio - bladder, urethra, genitals, descending colon, prostate gland, testes, sigmoid colon, nasal bone, pubic bone, red coloring matter in blood.
- Ophiuchus – fetal cells, tailbone, cranial sacral axis, solar sacrum, kundalini, amrita, lyden gland, base of brain (golden chalice), lunar to solar transfiguration.
- Sagittarius – hips, thighs, femur, ileum, coccygeal vertebrae, sacral region, sciatic nerves, pelvic ischium.
- Capricorn – skin, hair, knees, joints, skeletal system.
- Aquarius – ankles, lower limbs, circulatory system.
- Pisces – feet, toes, lymphatic system, adipose tissue, fibrin in blood, pancreas.

Structural principles are both energetic and geometric blueprints. Originally, Lunar Zodiacal Imprints were created by invading races to suppress human consciousness through the Lunar Matrix. However, this matrix is now being dismantled and realigned with the Natural Laws of God, hosted by the Aurora Ray System in Andromeda during the planetary Ascension Cycle.

Superhero Insight: Triune Timelines

Triune Sections (consists of three sections) - the opening in these timelines is called the Transtime Continuum Convergence:
1. Particle Universal Scale of Time
2. Anti-Particle Universal Scale of Time
3. Universal Inner Worlds Scale of Time (In-between Spaces)

Accumulation of Timelines
- As the planet accesses its memories, Triune Timelines accumulate.
- There are 864 Timelines, each representing a Time Vector Code.
  - Are Time Codes which manifest coordinate locations in dimensional spaces in timelines (time vectors).
- Together, they provide access to 1728 Christos Identities.

Superhero Insight: Time Vectors

Time Vectors - are time codes related to fire codes or fire letters, which are crucial for activating planetary and human DNA.

Activation and Shifting Timelines
When fire codes in DNA are activated, you can:
- Shift timelines
- Bypass timelines
- Eliminate destructive timelines
- Remember or view cellular memories from other timelines.
- Each DNA strand aligns with a Fire Letter or Fire Code, created by electromagnetic sound patterns.

Rehabilitation of Timelines
- Observing cellular memories from another timeline allows you to change or clear past choices that impacted the past, present, or future.
- This process is known as "rehabilitation of the timeline," which repairs genetic damage caused by the time vector code holding those historical records.
- **Color Correction** - Many of us are undergoing color correction to our Ray bodies, adjusting distortions from past timelines.

Astrological Precession rounded to 26,000 year cycles for easier charting. Use this as a guideline only.
- **Refer to table on next page, thanks to Lisa Renee @EnergeticSynthesis.Com**

Particle Timelines
- Our external reality on 3D Earth, encompassing 288 organic timelines.

Parallel Universe Timelines
- An antiparticle mirror of our universe with 288 additional organic timelines, totaling 576 timelines.

Universal Inner Worlds Scale of Time
- **In-between Spaces:** Intersecting domain of Particle and Anti-Particle Universes. It holds both sets of timelines and their cellular memories.
- **Accessible Timelines:** Includes 288 timelines from the Inner Worlds, totaling 864 timelines.

Simultaneous Planetary Time Cycles (12 Planetary Time Cycles in Triune Universal Scale)	Rounded Time Cycle 26,000	Triune 1 Timelines 24	Triune 2 Timelines 24	Triune 3 Timelines 24	Dimensionalized Identity Stations 12	Personal Christos Identities 144
1 1st Astrological Precession - Ending Current Cycle 2012	26,000	24	48	72	12	144
2 2nd Astrological Precession - Partial Ascension Cycle	52,000	48	96	144	24	288
3 3rd Astrological Precession - Partial Ascension Cycle	78,000	72	144	216	36	432
4 4th Astrological Precession - Partial Ascension Cycle	104,000	96	192	288	48	576
5 5th Astrological Precession - No Ascension Cycle	130,000	120	240	360	60	720
6 6th Astrological Precession - No Ascension Cycle	156,000	144	288	432	72	864
7 7th Astrological Precession - No Ascension Cycle	182,000	168	336	504	84	1008
8 8th Astrological Precession - Orion Invasion Causal Event**	208,000	192	384	576	96	1152
9 9th Astrological Precession - Universal Ascension	234,000	216	432	648	108	1296
10 10th Astrological Precession - Universal Ascension	260,000	240	480	720	120	1440
11 11th Astrological Precession - Universal Ascension	286,000	264	528	792	132	1584
12 12th Astrological Precession - Founder Cosmic Cube***	312,000	288	576	864	144	1728

Timeline Merges and New Architecture

Creation and Impact: New architecture emerges during timeline merges, affecting both particle and antiparticle time fields. This time is now.

Impact of Color Correction: Color correction and frequency saturation change cellular memories and shift timelines by altering events that caused distortions or genetic damage to our consciousness bodies.

ASCENSION PLAN B
PLUS MISSION UPGRADES SINCE 2005

Guardian Consciousness is the Celestial Management System – The Architects of Creation. They exist in both Incarnate and Disincarnate States of Being. They only perform function in accordance to the Law of One and Divine Will of Source Intelligence.

- Inner Templar and Organic Stargates Closed. No 5D Ascension. Accelerated Ascension Plan B to Incension through the Inner Hub Gate "Arc System" Networks. Mother Arc is the 13th Gateway.
- Accelerated Planetary Intelligence Realignments, Each Dimension systematically since 2005 to align to Inner Hub and Hosting Out Networks. The Aurora Guardian Families from Andromeda Core Matrix of the next Universe are hosting our Planet.
- Guardian Assignment to facilitate 12 D base pulse overrides to Planetary 10D Reversal Currents. Attempt to build as many 12D Hubs as possible to repair grids.
- Build as many transit stations through Transharmonic Pillar Gateways anchored into the more stable fields of the planetary body. Prepare for possible evacuation and portal jumping.
- Repair and erase Trigger Event Timelines in the cellular memory that create Cataclysmic Event Horizons due to Reptilian Agenda. (Ex: 911 Timeline, Reptile Invasion Timeline from Atlantis)
- Soul Matrix triad is the Current Focus of Repair, Rehabilitation and Reconnection. (4-5-6D)
- We are in the Now Presence of Zero (Eternal Time) - anything can happen in the miracle of God consciousness.

** EnergeticSynthesis.Com

This was not our first attempt at Ascension on Earth:

- The 5D Ascension was originally planned as Earth's evolutionary path, meant to occur at the end of the 2012 timelines or the Ascension Cycle. This plan aimed to merge Earth's 3D reality with its future 5D counterpart, known as Planet Tara.
- However, due to significant damage to Earth's consciousness fields caused by alien interference, mind control, and other negative influences, the original plan was abandoned.
- This damage included soul fragmentation and disconnection from spiritual sources, making it unsafe to activate Earth's inner Stargates, many of which were under hostile control.

Ascension Plan B was devised:

- As a result, the Krystal Star Guardians and Aurora Guardians shifted to a new mission, called Ascension Plan B.
- This plan focuses on repairing Earth's energetic architecture and addressing issues like alien machinery, false ascension systems, and other distortions.
- New structures, such as the Trinity Wave, were developed to heal these damages and support humanity's spiritual evolution.

- **The Trinity Wave** is accessed by merging masculine and feminine energies. Our species has been suppressed by Bi-Wave Influences that split gender polarity, making it impossible to connect to God Source through the sacred union of male and female. Sacred Union is our divine birthright, and this organic architecture is being restored during the Ascension Cycle as Hieros Gamos. The gender polarity pattern is changing on our planet, allowing us to access a new Trinity Wave or unity code through the embodiment of male "Rod" and female "Staff" energies.

- The shift also required reassembling councils and adjusting strategies to help souls transition and expand consciousness. However, the Negative Alien Agenda (NAA) continues to spread confusion and manipulation, often targeting spiritually gifted individuals like Indigos.
- Their aim is to derail progress by creating disinformation and recruiting individuals to mislead others.
- The challenges of mind control, trauma, and emotional wounds make it difficult for many humans to perceive reality clearly.
- Overcoming these barriers requires disciplined self-awareness, psychic defense training, and mental clarity. While negative influences, such as imposter spirits, may still pose threats, developing inner strength and spiritual mastery can help individuals resist manipulation and reclaim their freedom.

How to Identify them - Be careful who you follow:
- They violate the LAW OF ONE
- They charge subscriptions
- They usually sensationalize and have a large following
- They enjoy being in the public's eye - Energy Vampires

Recoding Bi-wave to Trinity Wave Guardian Assignments include Starseed couplings have been a work in progress in the planetary field architecture since February of 2009 to sequentially dismantle the polarity(bi-wave) of the Vesica Pisces harness and the NRG program headquartered in the United Kingdom.   ** EnergeticSynthesis.Com

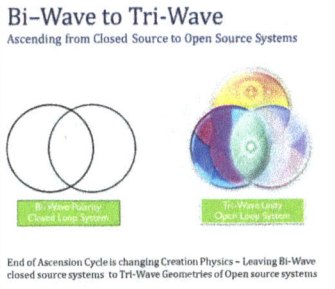

Bi-Wave to Tri-Wave
Ascending from Closed Source to Open Source Systems

End of Ascension Cycle is changing Creation Physics – Leaving Bi-Wave closed source systems to Tri-Wave Geometries of Open source systems

Simplified Insight: Ascension Plan B

Original Plan	5D Ascension Plan for Earth aborted
New Plan	Ascension Plan B by Aurora Guardians and Krystal Star
Reason for Change	Damaged consciousness fields, Alien Machinery, Dead Light, Bi-Wave Influences, NAA invasion, Mind Control, Alien Implants
Effects	Soul Fragmentation, disconnection from spiritual source, danger in opening inner Stargates
New Mission	Aurora Guardians and Krystal Star building Trinity Wave architecture to handle consciousness issues and repair energetic damage
Original Goal	Merge 3D Earth with parallel 5D Earth (Tara)

LAW OF ONE:

1. Unity Consciousness
2. Love Yourself
3. Love Others
4. Love Earth & Nature
5. Service to Others
6. Consciousness Expansion
7. Responsible Co-Creation

Superhero Code: The Law of One

The Law of One is the ultimate superhero code. It teaches that everything in the universe is interconnected and part of a single divine source. Here's a quick breakdown:
- **Unity** - All beings, energies, and things are interconnected and part of one universal consciousness.
- **Love and Compassion** - Embrace love, compassion, and understanding for yourself and others.
- **Service to Others** - Focus on helping others, promoting harmony, and elevating collective consciousness.
- **Integrity and Truth** - Live in alignment with your highest self, embodying honesty, transparency, and clarity.

Embrace the Law of One on your superhero journey, uniting with the universe and elevating your consciousness!

To practice the Law of One is to be "Compassion in Action," harmonizing our relationships with ourselves and others.

Basic Principles of Service to Others:
- **Unconditional Love:** See love in all things and extend compassion to everyone.
- **Spiritual Growth:** Dedicate yourself to personal and others' spiritual development.
- **Transform Ego:** Replace negative ego thoughts with positive behavior modeling.
- **Share Knowledge:** Openly share information and cooperate with others.
- **Beyond Material Needs:** Let go of materialistic ego needs.
- **Acknowledge Paths:** Recognize that everyone is on their own spiritual journey.
- **World Humanism:** Strive for a positive shared reality on Earth.

Nine Steps to Superhero Mastery under the LAW OF ONE:

Self-Responsibility: Own your emotional conflicts without blaming others. Reflect on forgiveness and resolve inner fears.

Conservation: Use your energy wisely. Avoid engaging in emotional dramas that scatter your focus.

Respond: Choose your responses consciously instead of reacting impulsively. Practice forgiveness, kindness, and self-love.

Reverence: Respect all beings' right to exist. Avoid harmful behaviors and let live.

Humility: Know your place in the universe. Serve without feeling superior or entitled.

Discernment: Test the resonance of people and events. Uphold personal boundaries and focus on what supports your growth.

Direct Knowing: Feel the energy and information in the present moment. Trust your intuitive insights.

Surrender: Let go of judgments and future expectations. Accept the lessons in every situation with unconditional love.

Be True to You: Honor yourself and your life force. Engage in activities that bring you joy and align with your higher purpose. Boundaries!!!

Embrace these steps and unlock your superhero potential, creating a harmonious and enlightened path ahead!

Superhero Insight: Navigating the New Dimensional Law

Profound Sadness
- Starseeds and Indigos may feel profound sadness as some human family members can't adapt to the new Law and will exit this dimension.

Spiritual Expansion
- At death, they'll move to another planet for continued spiritual growth or rehabilitation.
- We hoped they could stay on Earth for this journey, but it's not always possible.

Monadic Plane Visits
- Most at the Monadic plane level and beyond can visit their human families in new locations, though the reverse isn't possible.

Crossroads of Our Journey
- We're now governed by the new dimensional law.
- This designation will become clear, and soul growth will resume after death.
- The eventual outcome for most beings is joyful, with spiritual ascension and expanded consciousness becoming a reality for the masses and learning Service to Others as a Law of God.

Superhero Insight: Structural Changes in the Morphogenetic Field

Lightbody Grounding Platforms
- The morphogenetic field has created new platforms for grounding the light body, used by various soul groups in human tribes.
- These are included in the bifurcated layers of the earth realm.

Access and Synchronization
- Each person's access to timeline fields depends on their frequency, blueprint, and consciousness embodiment levels.
- Groups are synchronized into specific frequency areas within earth's collective consciousness fields.

Complex Planetary Interface
- The way energy is fed into individuals has become more complex, altering mass collective energy distribution and manifestation.

New Grounding Locations – This shift requires our body and consciousness to adjust to new grounding locations and energetic changes.

RECOGNIZING CO-DEPENDENCY

Superhero Insight: Identifying Co-Dependent Relationships
Spot the Signs of Co-Dependency

- Co-dependent relationships come disguised as sources of help and support, but they subtly strip away your power.
- You begin to rely heavily on them, and before you know it, you've surrendered your autonomy.
- These relationships require your consent, making you feel like you have no choice but to comply. Over time, you become addicted, unable to break free from their grip.

The Sneaky Matrix
- These co-dependent ties are like a tangled web spun by the matrix—be it healthcare systems, energy healers, the education system, processed food, organized religion, discrimination, government licenses, occult influences, or political strategies aimed at control, like the division between vaccinated and unvaccinated.
- These systems thrive on your dependency, feeding off your energy, and keeping you trapped.

Surrendering Your Power
- By giving in to these systems, you hand over your personal power. You allow them to dictate your choices and influence your well-being. This leads to a loss of self and an erosion of your inner strength.

Addiction and Consent
- Co-dependency is an addiction.
- It starts with small agreements, requiring your consent at each step, until you find yourself bound and unable to break free.
- They make you believe you need them, but in reality, you're losing your independence.

Dividing the Collective
- These systems also create division among the human collective, fostering fear, mistrust, and separation.
- By keeping people divided, they maintain control and infringe on your sovereignty.

Beware of Fake Lightworkers
- Just like fluorescent lights pretend to be true light but are harmful, so do fake lightworkers.
- Those who charge money for their services, promising to clear your chakras, blockages, or solve your problems, are energy vampires. They violate the Law of One by impeding your ascension and preventing you from doing your own healing and self-work.

- Additionally, their goal isn't to heal you but to keep you dependent on their services—just like doctors who ensure you need ongoing treatments. Ask yourself: Why don't they teach you to heal yourself?
- Escape this matrix to become your own superhero, instead of seeking quick fixes that don't work. Knowledge is POWER!
- Live with integrity and stay true to the principles of the Law of One. Never let money and power sway you like the fake lightworkers. Be ethical, transparent, and compassionate in all your actions.
- How can someone justify padding their pockets to live in 5D while enslaving their brothers and sisters in 3D jobs to pay for your services? This violates the Law of One and impedes true ascension.
- Instead, focus on empowering others to become their own superheroes, breaking free from dependency and embracing their own healing and self-work.
- Channel your energy into organic and natural remedies. Focus on clearing your lower chakras, and dive into the world of bio plasma cell salts that heal various ailments.
  - For further information refer to the book **Ascension Classified Intel** by Lisa Renee, Section on Bioplasma Cell Salts, pages 77-88.

Break Free and Rise
- Recognizing these signs is the first step to breaking free.
- As you identify the chains that bind you, you can reclaim your power, foster unity, and expand your consciousness. Embrace your superhero strength and rise above these limitations.
- Educate yourself about the influences and tactics used to control you. Knowledge is power, and it equips you to resist manipulation.

Harness your inner superhero power by identifying and breaking free from co-dependent relationships.

TAKE BACK YOUR POWER *and soar to new heights!*

Superhero Insight: The Universal Matrix and Akashic Records

Unlocking the Universal Matrix
- The Universal Matrix of Cellular Memory contains every recorded event and experience across our 15-dimensional Universal Time Matrix.
- This sacred science explains Christ Consciousness and the natural laws governing the universe.

Akashic Records
- Also known as the "Akasha," the Akashic Records are our Universal God Seed Code system, holding all frequencies and codes that created our universe.
- The Guardians call this the "Eckasha" or Ecka Universal System.
- When we do emotional clearing work, we often declare our sovereignty by commanding the clearance of trauma from our "Akashic Record," freeing our holographic energy field across all time and space.

Halls of Records
- On a planetary and solar level, the Halls of Records are like immersive theaters where you can witness existence across all time frames if your body can pass through Stargates.
- When your lightbody connects to the Cosmic Spirit Body, you achieve entrance into the Cosminya Hall of Records, holding the divine blueprint of organic creation according to the Natural Laws of God.

Ancient References
- The Akashic Records, Hall of Records, or the Eternal Book of Life are mentioned in many sacred texts.
- These records, emanating from the primordial substance of the Eternal God Source, project as the DNA record of all creation over time.

Cosmic Cluster
- In the highest core of the Godhead, within the central cosmic matrix, lies the eternal seven suns and the hidden Eighth Sun.

Cosmic Convergence
- As universal time cycles converge, the cosmic records of Cosminya open to authentic Ascended Masters, revealing the entire cosmic memory matrix.

Connecting to the Cosmic Spirit Body
- When your lightbody connects to the Cosmic Spirit Body, you reach the ultimate ascension initiation.
- This opens the Cosminya Hall of Records, which holds the divine blueprint of organic creation according to the Natural Laws of God.

Stages of Access
- Access to the Akashic Records requires purity and ethical standards.
- Those with selfish motivations or negative ego desires can only attain **partial or corrupted views.**
- With a pure heart and sacred intent, one can request *access to* **their own** *Akashic record to view past life patterns and clear emotional pain.*

Ethical Path to Access
- Rudolf Steiner described a path of inner development, requiring rigorous ethical and cognitive self-discipline, concentration, and meditation.
- Moral development must precede spiritual faculties to access the true Akashic Records.

Guardians of the Records
- The Melchizedek Logos and Emerald Founders, along with the Maharaji groups, are safeguarding the natural memory matrix of our universe.
- They determine what is artificial and organic, moving authentic records to the safekeeping of Cosmic Christos Suns, Blue Ray Melchizedek archivists, and Emerald Dragon Timekeepers.
  - Reference: EnergeticSynthesis.Com

If you're paying some GURU to look up your records, please use discernment and re-read the above.

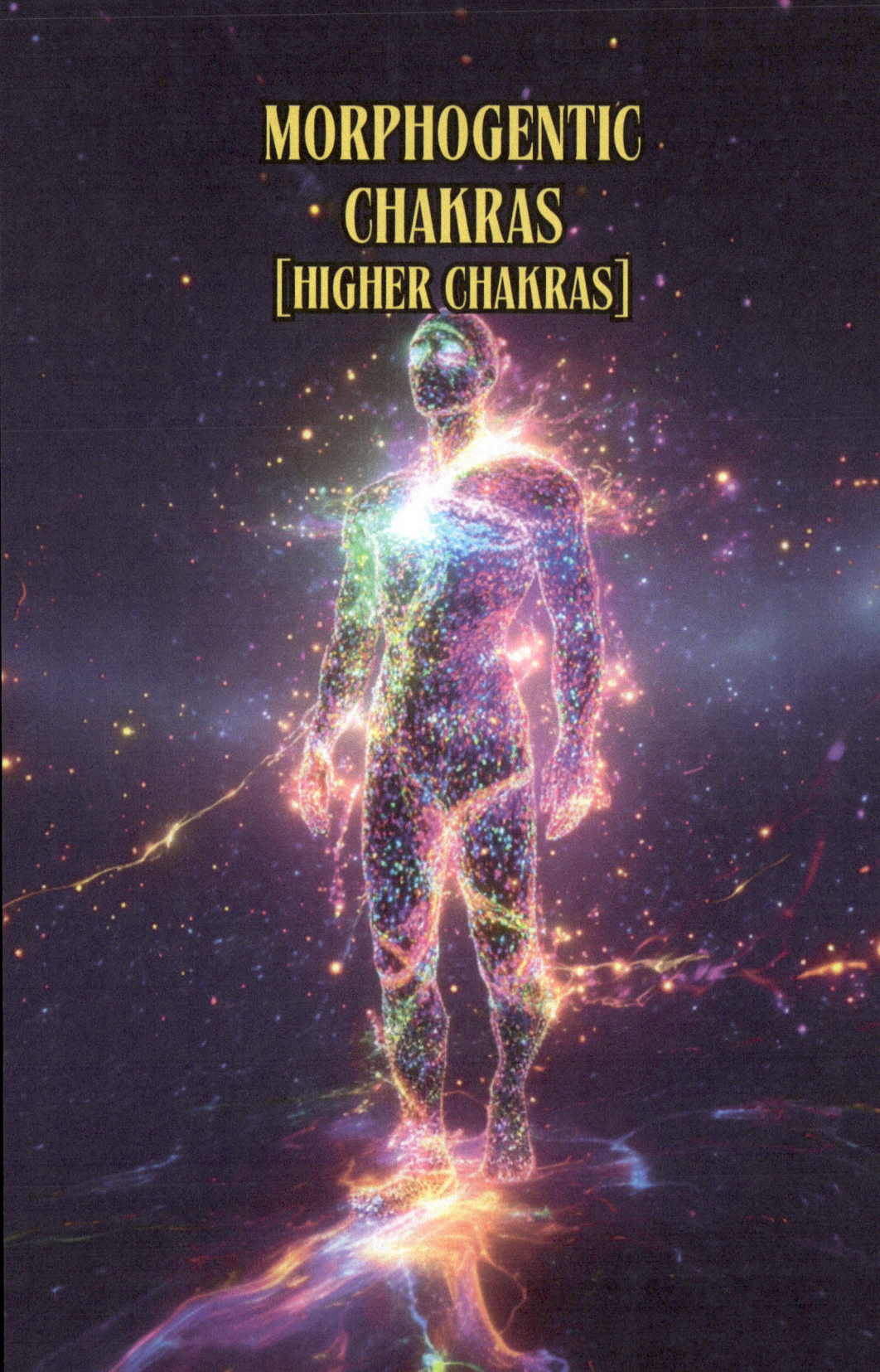

Superhero Evolution: Morphogenetic Chakras

In advanced spiritual development, the particle and antiparticle (morphogenetic) chakras merge into a single Unified Column through Monadic Integration.
- This represents the unification of male and female chakras, creating unity consciousness.

Morphogenetic Chakras (8-15)
8th Chakra: Higher Heart Chakra
9th Chakra: Atomic Doorway
10th Chakra: Solar Star
11th Chakra: Galactic Chakra
12th Chakra: Earth Star
13th Chakra: Earth Core or Universal Mother Chakra
14th Chakra: Universal Sun Chakra
15th Chakra: Universal Father Chakra

Unity Consciousness
The Unified Column evolves into the highest state of consciousness, known as the Krystala orb body. **MERKABA**

Superhero Spaceship: The Krystala Orb Body

This is a highly advanced state of spiritual embodiment, representing the merging of male and female energy centers into a unified light body.
Powerful Energy Field futuristic & beyond comprehension.

Superhero Soul: Embrace Your Cosmic Blueprint

Origin of Your Soul
- Every Soul is like a unique superhero, originating from the Eternal God Source (Infinite Consciousness).
- Each Soul has a special blueprint with a divine purpose: to learn, evolve, experience all aspects of creation, and eventually return to reunite with the God Source.

Soul Body Superpowers
- Your Soul body holds three superpowers: creative imagination, receptivity, and feeling perception.
- It stores all your memories from various lifetimes, embedding them into your body's cellular matrix. This repository of experiences helps shape your internal reality.

Soul Connection
- Without a connected Soul body, your powers and memories get distorted or blocked.
- The Soul is your higher sensory body, enabling you to experience deep emotions and feelings.
- It also acts as a bridge to your Monad body and Inner Holy Spirit, igniting your Higher Heart (thymus area)

Soul Matrix - 2nd Harmonic Universe

- The Soul Matrix is the starting point of your spiritual journey, where you connect and integrate your Soul energies and heart complex.
- Made up of three layers (4D, 5D, 6D), each layer correlates with a chakra, a colored wave spectrum, and a dimension of time and space in the future.

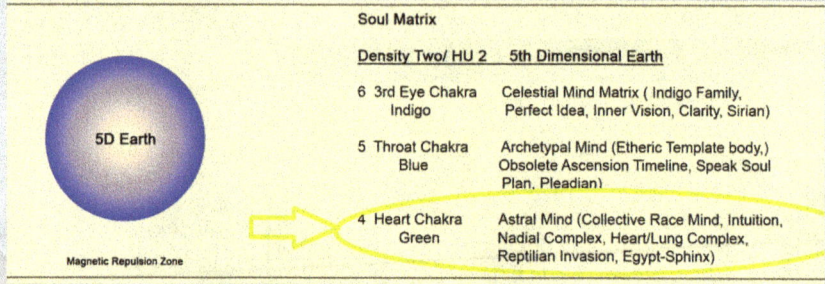

** Graph from Energeticsynthesis.com

Superhero's Guide to the 4th Chakra Layer

Your Heart Intelligence

- The 4th layer of your chakra system is where you tap into your divinity. This is home to your soul matrix and heart intelligence, the core of your superhero spirit.
- 4th Layer of the Lightbody
- This layer of your Lightbody is connected to the 4th layer of the planet's lightbody, known as the Astral Plane.
- This connection opens up powerful energies that influence your heart and soul.

Astral Plane Gateway

- The gateway to the Astral Plane is the 4th Dimensional Planetary Stargate, located at Giza in Egypt.
- This Stargate acts as a portal, leading you into the deeper layers of the Astral Plane, where your heart intelligence and soul matrix thrive.

Why is the 4th Chakra important?

- The Monad spiritual body triad is the 7th, 8th and 9th layer but it starts connecting at the 8th Chakra level (Thymus) which is the Higher Heart.
- When the Monad starts coming in like this, the whole Heart changes pattern, meaning the Heart Chakra is no longer an Astral Heart 4th Chakra, it is a Blue Heart.
- Again, it is a process, there are no short cuts, and you cannot pay someone to do it for you. NO Guru$.

Superhero Transformation: Embrace the Upgrade

- Imagine still using an old rotary landline phone while everyone else is rocking the latest smartphones.
- Sure, your landline has nostalgia, but it's stuck in one place, tethered by cords and offering limited features.
- Meanwhile, smartphones let you carry the world in your pocket—photos, videos, apps, navigation, and instant communication anywhere!
- Why keep that old landline?
- Upgrading is like trading your landline for a state-of-the-art superhero gadget that connects you to the universe.
- Your chakras are evolving, merging into a powerful unified light channel, just like moving from the confines of a landline to the freedom of a smartphone.

And that's okay, those that are not ready for these upgrades or who have not integrated their chakras will not do so. There are no shortcuts to this process.

Superhero Soul Integration - Unlock Your Multidimensional Powers

Soul and Monad:
- Your Superfamily of Consciousness
- Your Soul and Monad are like a superhero family, with extensions existing in different dimensions and timelines.

First Level of Awakening
- The first step in your spiritual journey is connecting with your soul consciousness and its extensions.
- Your soul family includes 12 unique personalities.
- As you integrate these aspects, your consciousness body unifies, and you start experiencing emotions and love in powerful new ways.

Complete Soul Integration
- Reaching full soul integration takes you to the next level—integrating with your Monadic or Oversoul Matrix.
- This matrix contains 12 oversouls, each with 12 souls, totaling 144 extensions. [Refer to 144 Soul Extensions (Monad), pages 163-168]
- Each stage of integration significantly expands your consciousness, connecting you to everything and revealing a Universe filled with endless possibilities.

Accelerated Integration
- Right now, the process of soul extension and monadic family reintegration is happening faster than ever, thanks to the shift into organic timelines.

Superhero Adventure: Emotional Liberation

Release Blockages
- Free yourself from emotional blockages and past traumas, breaking away from limiting patterns and beliefs.

Inner Peace
- Experience profound inner peace and emotional balance, living more authentically and joyfully.

Embrace Transformation
- Your spiritual progress and evolution are signs of stepping into a new realm of potential and enlightenment. Become a more empowered, vibrant, and spiritually attuned version of yourself.

Exciting Journey: Chakra Balance Through the Hara Line

- **Get Comfortable**
  - Imagine gearing up for an epic adventure. Sit with your spine straight, close your eyes, and take deep, calming breaths. Feel your body relax as you prepare for this journey.

- **Focus on Your Hara Line**
  - Visualize a glowing line of energy starting two inches below your navel, running straight down into the earth and extending upward through your body.

- **Dive Into the Earth**
  - Imagine the Hara line as a magical tunnel diving deep into the earth. Check for blockages or imbalances, ensuring the energy flow is clear and grounded.

- **Ascend to the Stars**
  - Shift your focus upward along the Hara line, traveling through your body to the crown of your head. Check for balanced and free-flowing energy, rising into the cosmos and aligning with the stars.

- **Restore Balance**
  - Visualize a bright, cleansing light flowing through any blockages or imbalances, restoring energy flow.
  - Imagine yourself as a powerful sorcerer, casting a spell of harmony and balance.

- **Take a Final Deep Breath**
  - Take a deep breath, feeling alignment and balance throughout your body. Gently open your eyes, feeling centered and harmonious, with newfound clarity and peace.

Superhero's Guide to Chakra Mastery Daily Balance
- Balancing and clearing your chakras daily is like polishing your superhero armor.
- Embrace the sun and ground yourself with Earth's energy to harness your higher consciousness.

Cosmic Power Source
- The sun is your cosmic power source, supercharging your abilities.
- Discover the ultimate starseed supplement and lower chakra troubleshooting techniques in my previous book *Ascension Classified Intel*, your superhero manual for unlocking and maintaining your full potential.

Remember, superheroes, keeping those chakras aligned and powered up is key to unlocking your cosmic consciousness and living your best superpowered life!

It is important to know that if your lower chakras have a block and are not balanced, you cannot access the higher chakras.

Superhero Reflection: Cosmic Responsibility

The Cosmic Keyholder
- Would the universe entrust an unbalanced, egomaniac with the keys to the kingdom? The universe, in all its wisdom, grants extraordinary powers to those who embody balance, humility, and self-awareness. True superheroes are chosen not just for their abilities, but for their unwavering commitment to justice, empathy, and harmony.
- These powers demand a hero who understands the weight of their actions and strives to uplift others.

Cosmic Responsibility
- The universe seeks guardians who will use their gifts to protect, heal, and inspire.
- It's a sacred trust, a mission to bring light to darkness and balance to chaos. Remember, true superhero status comes not from power alone, but from the wisdom and heart to use it for the greater good.

Uplifting Journey Through the Higher Chakras

Are you ready to take a cosmic joyride through the higher chakras? Buckle up, Guardian of the New Earth! This is going to be a wild, enlightening adventure filled with laughs and aha moments!

8th Chakra
Your Higher Heart
The Soul Star Chakra

Location: About 6-12 inches above your head.
Color: Gold, like the glittery crown of a cosmic being.
Function: Connects you to divine wisdom and your higher self.
Think of it as your superhero headquarters where you receive all the cosmic intel.

Activating Your Superhuman Monad Spirit Body

Gear Up, Superhuman! Let's make this journey exciting and easy to understand. Here's how to unlock your Monad spirit body and unleash your superhuman abilities:

Activate Your Power Center (8th Chakra)
- Start with the 8th Chakra, located at your thymus gland (upper chest). This is like turning on your superhero control center for higher energy.

Power Up the Seed Atom
- When the Permanent Seed Atom activates, it kickstarts the integration process. Think of it as powering up your core energy source, ready to boost your superhuman potential.

Link with the 9th Chakra
- The Seed Atom connects with your 9th Chakra, creating a moving energy field centered in your Pineal Gland (middle of the brain). This field helps stabilize and distribute energy, like a superhuman energy grid.

Ignite the Amoraea Flame
- The Amoraea Flame lights up when you connect the three layers of your soul into one unified body. This flame is your Inner Holy Spirit, residing in the higher heart complex (8th Chakra at the thymus gland). It's like lighting your superhuman beacon!

Superhero Awakening: Activating the Monad Spirit Body

8th Chakra Activation
- The Monad spirit body activates with the 8th Chakra at the thymus gland. This triggers the Permanent Seed Atom, linking with the 9th Chakra in a gyroscopic field centered at the pineal gland.

Monadic Integration
- As bodies merge, the mental trinity awakens new sensory functions, enabling shapeshifting and projecting consciousness into other dimensions.

Teuric Shield [Stellar Guardian Shield]
- The Teuric Shield holds 7D-8D-9D DNA layers, chakras, and seed crystals forming three mental bodies in the third Harmonic Universe: 7D Ketheric Mind, 8D Monadic, and 9D Keriatric Minds.

Building the Teuric Shield
- Through Monadic integration, we build the Teuric Shield, evolving our consciousness.

9th Chakra: Mouth of God
- The 9th Chakra, at the back of the neck, connects to the Medulla Oblongata, reticular formation, and the Silver Cord in the Crown, holding the "Golden Chalice" of Universal Knowledge.

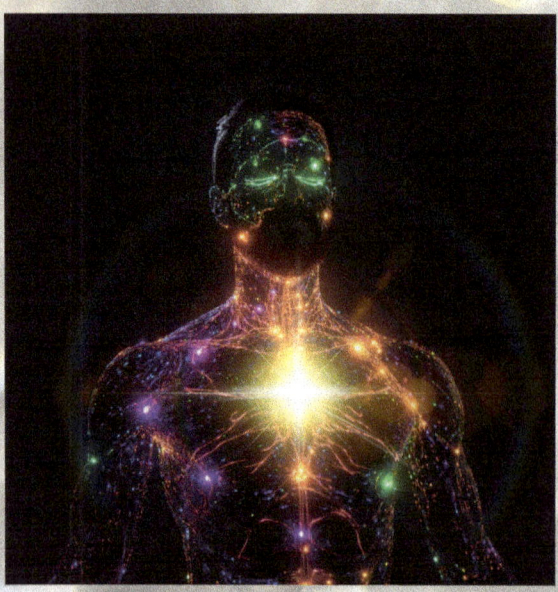

The Monad spiritual body triad is the 7th, 8th and 9th layer but it starts connecting at the 8th Chakra level (Thymus) which is the Higher Heart.

When the Monad starts coming in like this, the whole Heart changes pattern, meaning the Heart Chakra is no longer an Astral Heart 4th Chakra, it is a Blue Heart.

Universal Knowledge
- We're connecting to new layers of knowledge, feeling changes in our "field" and relationships.

Alta Major Center
- Located at the base of the skull, this center, also known as the Mouth of God or Goddess, regulates brain and gland functions, connecting to the hara center where the Monadic identity anchors.

Trinity Circuit
- To communicate with the higher heart center at the thymus, three head energy centers (hypothalamus, pituitary, pineal) link, bringing spiritual blueprints into physical actualization. *Do you understand why it was so important to decalcify your pineal gland during the awakening process.?*

How to Detox your Pineal Gland: Incorporate foods like alfalfa sprouts, parsley, oregano oil, spirulina, coconut oil, walnuts, chlorophyll-rich foods, beets, apple cider vinegar, lemon water, lavender essential oil, turmeric, ginseng, and bentonite clay, and avoid processed foods with additives, preservatives, and chemicals. Natural sunlight, organic foods and avoid fluoride and BIG PHARM drugs. These are a few things that are helpful. This is an ongoing process as well.

Stations of Identity
- Human consciousness bodies exist throughout densities, called Stations of Identity, integrated through the Teuric Shield.

Evolving Beyond Earth
- As we integrate higher dimensions, our auric field and lightbody evolve, taking on new shapes, colors, and frequencies. We transition into a more expansive state, harmonizing with the galactic symphony and universal energy flow.

Activate the Higher Heart Complex
- This is where the Amoraea Flame resides, balancing and integrating higher energies. It prepares you to harness your superhuman powers.

Harmonize and Elevate
- By following these steps, you enhance your spiritual growth and connection to higher dimensions.

Superhero Meditation: Ignite the Amoraea Flame

Step into Your Power - *Your lower chakras must be completely balanced and supercharged for this!!*

- Sit or lie down in a comfortable, quiet place. Imagine you are in your superhero headquarters, a space of immense power and tranquility.

Ground Yourself (HEAVY GROUNDING PRIOR TO THIS)
- Close your eyes and take a deep breath in.
- Feel your connection to Earth, like roots anchoring you firmly. Exhale slowly, releasing any tension or negativity.

Activate Your Inner Light
- Visualize a glowing orb of light at your thymus gland (located at your chest, between your heart and throat).
- This is your Higher Heart Complex.

Summon the Amoraea Flame
- See this light transforming into a vibrant, swirling flame—the Amoraea Flame.
- Feel its warmth and energy expanding throughout your chest.

Left-Nose, Right-Nose Breath Exchange
- Close your right nostril with your right thumb and inhale deeply through your left nostril.
- Close your left nostril with your right pinky, release your right thumb, and exhale through your right nostril. Inhale again through your right nostril, then switch to exhale through your left.
- Continue this alternate breathing pattern for a few cycles to balance your energy.

Embrace Your Superpowers
- As the flame grows stronger, imagine it lighting up your entire body. Feel your energy amplifying, your senses sharpening, and your consciousness expanding.

Connect to the Galactic Symphony
- Visualize beams of light extending from your Higher Heart Complex to the stars, linking you to the galactic symphony. Feel the universal energy flowing through you, harmonizing your being.

Harness the Energy
- With each breath, draw this cosmic energy into your body, empowering the Amoraea Flame. (Like the wind fans a FLAME)
- Feel the energy igniting your superhuman potential, filling you with strength and purpose.

Affirm Your Power
- Silently or aloud, affirm:
  - "I am a beacon of light, connected to the universal flow."
  - "I harness the power of the Amoraea Flame to elevate my spirit and fulfill my cosmic mission."

Anchor the Flame
- Visualize the Amoraea Flame settling into your Higher Heart Complex, a constant source of power and guidance.
- Feel its presence, ready to be ignited whenever you need it.

Return to Earth
- Take a few deep breaths, feeling grounded yet energized.
- Open your eyes, knowing you have activated your inner superhero and are ready to embrace your mission.
- Make sure you document this event in your Journal.

Embrace this superhero meditation, ignite the Amoraea Flame, and unleash your cosmic potential!

Aqua Portal: Gateway of Cosmic Compassion

When the 8th Chakra is activated, it ignites the Amoraea Flame, a sacred connection to the Mother Arc—the divine frequency of the Holy Mother's love. This activation unlocks the ability to create the Aqua Portal, a powerful gateway for the transit of earthly souls and entities.

- Through this portal, they can be guided to the Mother's embrace for healing, rehabilitation, or higher-dimensional transit.
- This process is a direct embodiment of the Law of One, heralding the return of the Holy Mother's energy to Earth.

Becoming a Guardian of the Aqua Portal
- The Aqua Portal is reserved for those aligned with Service to Others and the Sacred Law of One.
- If this is your divine purpose, the Guardian Host may assist you in holding the portal, provided your body and consciousness are attuned to the 12D Shield.
- To independently hold this sacred space, one must demonstrate spiritual integrity and unwavering dedication to the Law of One. Through consistent effort, the 8th Chakra and higher heart awaken into the radiant Crystal Blue Lotus Heart, a gateway to the Transharmonic Gate of the Aqua Portal.

Your Cosmic Superpower
- As a steward of the Aqua Portal, you channel the Mother Arc's boundless compassion and serve as a bridge between worlds, offering souls the opportunity for healing and ascension.

Photo from EnergeticSynthesis.com

Superhero Insight: The Evolution of Earth

Aramatena and the Future Earth

- Aramatena is the 12th Lyran Stargate, representing the future Earth blueprint in its crystalline form within the Avatar Matrix Universe. I bet you were never taught this in your history books.

- The Aurora or Ascension Earth is located in the Andromedan. accessed through the passage connecting the Milky Way and Andromeda Galaxy and that is connected through the networks of the Polarian Gate hosting system.

- Different E.T. Races and extra dimensionals may call these future Earths by different names based on their language. (Such as Urantia) They are all planet Earth at different stages of evolution in the timelines.

Our planet exists in three main identities in this Universal Time Matrix:
- 3D Earth: Known as Earth or Terra.
- 5D Earth: Known as Tara.
- 7D Earth: Known as Gaia.

9th CHAKRA

9th Chakra
The Atomic Doorway - Projector of Light Consciousness

Location: Floating above the 8th Chakra.
Color: Reflective silver, like a shiny UFO.
Function: Known as the Mouth of God and is located at the back of the neck where the skull meets the spine. It connects to the Medulla Oblongata, the reticular formation of the brain and spinal cord, and the Silver Cord in the Crown, linking to the Threefold Founder Flame.

Links you to the galaxy's collective consciousness.
Imagine getting a galactic dispatch to help you save the universe!

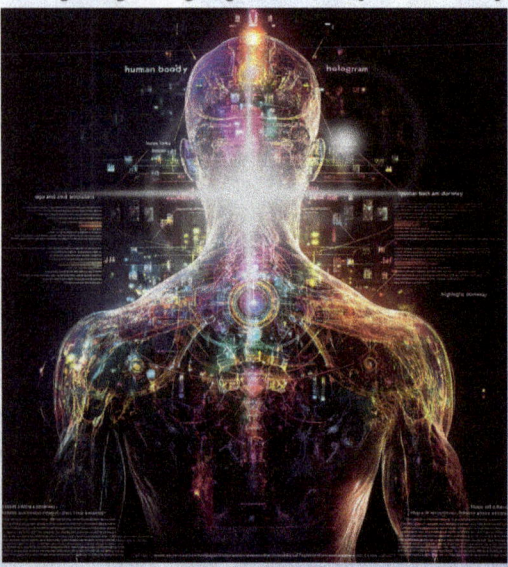

Superhero Commitment: Daily Chakra Mastery
Daily Dedication
- Releasing and clearing chakras isn't a one-time task. It's a daily commitment to operate in your higher chakras.
- Your Hara line must be white and perfectly balanced.
- Hopefully, you've started a journal documenting your progress.

Higher Heart Connection
- Maintains communication with the higher heart center (thymus gland) and builds the crystal lotus breath configuration in the Sacred Crystal Heart.

Communication with Monadic Consciousness
- This trinity circuit brings down monadic consciousness layers, translating spiritual blueprints through the throat center and voice box.

Spiritual Mission
- Allows conscious awareness of your deep heart expression and actualizes your personal spiritual mission on Earth.

Superhero Power-Up: The Ascension Chakra

Ascension Chakra (9th Morphogenetic Chakra)
- Also known as the Ascension Chakra, it connects to the Oversoul / Monad at 9D.
- Corresponds to the medulla oblongata and connects to the Universal Antahkarana (link between the middle and higher mind) current.
- Regulates brain and glandular functions, linking to the Hara center where the Monadic identity anchors.
- Many of us are becoming aware of a new "language," octave, or dimensional layer of knowledge. We're accelerating into spiritual body development, accessing Universal Knowledge from the Golden Chalice, activating processes in the base of our brain.

Location
- This Morphogenetic Chakra is at the back of the head where the neck meets the skull, acting as an energetic command center.

Atomic Doorway
- The 9th Chakra, or Atomic Doorway, projects God/Goddess Consciousness Units through the Medulla Oblongata at the base of your neck.

Thalamus: Your Brain's Relay Station
- The thalamus is a walnut-shaped structure at the center of the brain.
- It relays all sensory information (sight, sound, touch, smell, taste) to other brain parts.
- The thalamus processes all sensations, thoughts, and emotions, determining what's real.
- The thalamus doesn't differentiate between internal and external inputs.

Trinity Circuit
- Connects three main brain glands: Hypothalamus, Pituitary, and Pineal.
- Links the top of the head, forehead, and base of the skull.

Andromeda Energies
- These energies activate the 9th Dimensional Axiatonal Lines on the right side of your body, moving up to the 9th Chakra.

Silver Frequency
- The frequency is dull silver, running from your right toe, up through your right finger, to the base of your neck

Lightbody Activation
- When activated, this creates a microcosmic orbit with the 8th Chakra, forming a macrocosmic orbit with planetary kundalini forces.
- Picture a gyroscopic sphere of spiraling frequencies around your upper body and head.

Superhero Senses: Signs Your 9th Chakra is Activated

Heightened Spiritual Awareness
- You feel a stronger connection to higher dimensions and universal consciousness. Insights and spiritual wisdom come more naturally.

Clarity and Intuition
- Your intuition is sharper, and you often experience moments of clarity and knowing without logical reasoning.

Inner Peace and Serenity
- A deep sense of peace and tranquility fills your being, even in challenging situations.

Vivid Dreams and Astral Travel
- Your dreams become more vivid, and you may experience astral travel or out-of-body experiences.

Synchronistic Events
- You notice an increase in synchronicities, where events align in meaningful ways, guiding you on your path.

Expanded Awareness
- You have a broader perspective on life and feel a sense of oneness with all beings.

Energy Sensations
- You might feel tingling or warmth at the back of your head or upper neck, indicating an energetic activation.

Connection to Divine Wisdom
- You receive messages and guidance from higher realms more frequently, and your understanding of spiritual concepts deepens.
- Feel these superhero signs and know that your 9th Chakra is activated, bringing you closer to your higher self and cosmic wisdom!

When it comes to opening these chakras, it's generally recommended to focus on one chakra at a time to ensure proper alignment and integration. Opening too many at once can be overwhelming and may lead to energetic imbalances.

10th Chakra
The Solar Star Chakra

Location: 6 inches above the crown, the Solar Star Chakra is a brilliant sapphire color.
Function: Aligns you with solar energies and higher spiritual frequencies.

Picture yourself soaking up the sun's energy, powering up like a superhero on a solar charge!

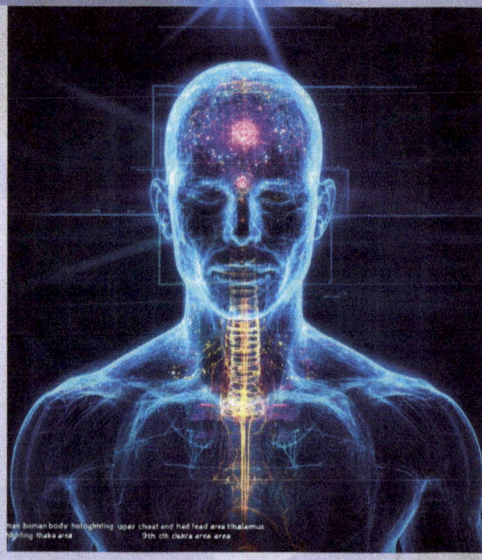

10th Chakra Connections
Lines run around the left side of your body, connecting from behind the left ear to the crown chakra and into the Soul Star above your head.

- This chakra acts as a communication hub for your Avatar (triad) Christ consciousness intelligence.
- Without it, you can't sense communication at that frequency.

Decode the Language
- The 10th Chakra and 10th Axiatonal Lines form the network in your Lightbody that decodes and senses this communication within your own body.
- Activate your 10th Chakra, unlock the communication hub, and enhance your superhero abilities to sense cosmic messages!

Superhero Connection: The 10th Chakra
10th Chakra Network
- The 10th Chakra lines run along the left side of your body, with the main portal connecting from behind the left ear to the crown and then to the Soul Star, 6-8 inches above your head.

Superhero Power: Morphogenetic Chakras

Higher Spiritual Development
- Begins at Monadic Integration.

Unified Column
- Morphogenetic Chakras (8-15) merge particle and antiparticle into one unified column.

Gender Unification
- This process unifies male and female principle chakras, creating a unified consciousness column.

Superhero Insight: The Aton Solar Disk

Aton Solar Disk Activation
- During the Ascension Cycle, the Aton Solar Disk becomes an embodied shield in the Starseeded and human Lightbody.
- It integrates into the solar sacrum and Double Diamond Sun DNA Template.
- This disk, when activated into the 10-11-12D Solar Logos base shield, aligns with the 10D Solar Star above the head.
- As this energy restores, the crown shifts to the organic North Star, leading back to the God Worlds.

Aton God Body
- The Aton God Body operates through the Ankh Solar Lightbody, transferring and moving consciousness through portals.
- When embodied, it acts as the Transfiguration Vehicle or God Worlds Eternal Merkaba Vehicle.

Travel and Transformation
- The Aton Disk of Solar Christ Consciousness secures the energy needed to build the Solar Body and Aton of the Ankh.
- This allows the ascending human to travel through time or consciously transport themselves into other dimensions through meditation and consciousness transportation.

Superhero Insight: SunStar Networks

Bifurcation Event
In October 2023, the planet experienced a major Bifurcation event. The worlds separated between the 3D Lunar Matrix distortions and the newly aligned 5D Sun-Star Networks. The corrected solar calendar positions for ascending timelines are now in place, with no turning back.

Higher Timeline Positions
These higher timeline sun star networks anchor into the trifurcated section.

Superhero Insight: Trifurcation
We used to talk about bifurcation (splitting into two). Now, there's a new split—trifurcation—into three sections:
- Three Split Realities
- Original Split Sections: Two familiar sections.
- New Third Section: A completely separate field, including the upper timelines of 9D and above, hosted by the Andromedan Aquaferion Shields (connected to the Blue Feather Family).

- <u>More simplified:</u>
  - **Superhero Insight: Trifurcation -** The higher zones of Logos to Rishi are being dimensionalized for Starseed Dragon people. This means our light body and plasma orb body are attuning to the 9D upper timelines.

  - **Key Points:**
    - **Upper Timelines (9D+):** Connected to Solar Logos and Rishi, meant for Starseed Dragon people and those aligned with Cosmic Christos Dragon and Emerald Order.
    - **Median Timelines (1D-5D):** Most people are on this timeline, undergoing mind control clearing and spiritual healing. This is the 5D ascension layer.
    - **Lower AI Timelines:** For those deeply involved in dark practices, this timeline involves the inorganic timewave and transhuman agenda.
    - See EnergeticSynthesis.Com for more information

Navigating the Timelines
- We'll coexist in these three timelines (trifurcation) simultaneously.
- Focus on aligning with God and organic consciousness to stay on the organic ascension timeline.

Remember
- The AI timeline won't consume the Earth—the war is over in higher realms.
- We're living through the routing of consciousness souls. No one is left behind. Some will ascend and some will descend in order to ascend.

* Only take what resonates with you *

Superhero Insight: Earth's Visible Areas

Higher Ascension Earth Timeline
- The Ascension Earth Star template includes all planetary consciousness, visible to those grounded in this platform.
- Access to Taran and Gaian bodies and Andromedan Matrix groups is available.
- This level has no lower chakras, only spherical morphogenetic centers (your higher chakras).
- It stabilizes and hosts all planetary field sections.

Median Earth Timeline
- The previous 3D earth reality now resides in a lower section of the Median Earth timeline.
- Most earth inhabitants' ground into this platform, transitioning from the old 3D Ray system to the new Aurora Ray system.
- Communication with departed loved ones may increase as dimensionalization shifts.

Hibernation Zones
- Used by the Negative Alien Agenda to sequester lost souls, these zones harvest life force energy. Trapped consciousness in these zones will be gradually retrieved by Guardian teams.

Inner Earth Timeline
- Inner Earth timelines allow access to Transharmonic fields and parallel realities.
- These timelines open connections to advanced inner earth residents, undergoing their own spiritual ascension. Surface dwellers may return to these timelines during the 3 day bardo.
  - The team "bardo" comes from Tibetan Buddhism and refers to the intermediate state between death and rebirth. The "3-day bardo" specifically refers to the initial period after death, during which the consciousness is believed to be in a transitional state.

AI Assimilation Earth Timeline
- The Negative Alien Agenda (NAA) desired timeline for control and harvesting lost souls, using AI-powered virtual realities.
- Inhabitants experience virtual realities, often unaware of the consciousness trap.
- This timeline promotes transhumanism and bio-tech methods.

Bifurcation and Consciousness Corridors
- The bifurcation outlines the Consciousness Corridors, indicating the future direction of individuals and their group consciousness frequency hubs, forming reality bubbles. These synchronize into holographic frequency containers on the earth grid.

Only take what is useful for your spiritual growth and discard the rest.

Thank you for your courage and bravery to be a truth seeker.

Superhero Mission: Activate the 10th Chakra

Step into Your Power-Up Zone

Go to your flight deck and sit in your Commander's Chair
- Sit comfortably in a quiet place. Imagine you're in your superhero command center, surrounded by powerful, positive energy.

Ground Yourself & make sure your Hara Line is WHITE
- Close your eyes and take deep breaths. Inhale deeply through your nose, hold for a moment, and exhale slowly through your mouth. Feel your body relaxing, ready to embark on this epic mission.

Visualize the Solar Star Chakra
- Picture a brilliant sapphire light about 6-8 inches above your head.
- This is your 10th Chakra—the Solar Star Chakra.

Activate the Triad Communication Station
- Imagine a network of energy lines connecting from behind your left ear, moving to your crown, and extending to the Soul Star above your head.
- Feel this network coming online, buzzing with energy.

Feel the Frequency
- Sense the dull silver frequency running up from your right toe, through your right finger, and into the base of your neck.
- This energy activates your 10th Chakra, linking it with the Thalamus.

Connect with the Avatar Consciousness
- Visualize your Avatar Christ consciousness sending messages through this communication hub.
- Feel the energy flowing, enhancing your awareness and connection.

Harmonize the Energies
- Picture the energies of the 8th and 10th Chakras forming a gyroscopic sphere of spiraling frequencies around your upper body and head.
- Feel these energies harmonizing and integrating within you.

Affirm Your Power
- Silently or aloud, affirm: "I activate my Solar Star Chakra, opening the channels of higher communication and cosmic awareness. I am connected, empowered, and enlightened."

Anchor the Energy
- Visualize the sapphire light of the Solar Star settling into place, a constant source of power and guidance.
- Feel this energy integrated within your Lightbody.
- Return to Earth Take a few deep breaths, grounding yourself back into the present moment.
- Open your eyes, feeling empowered and ready to embrace your superhero potential.

Your lower chakras must be balanced, cleared and membranes dissolved.

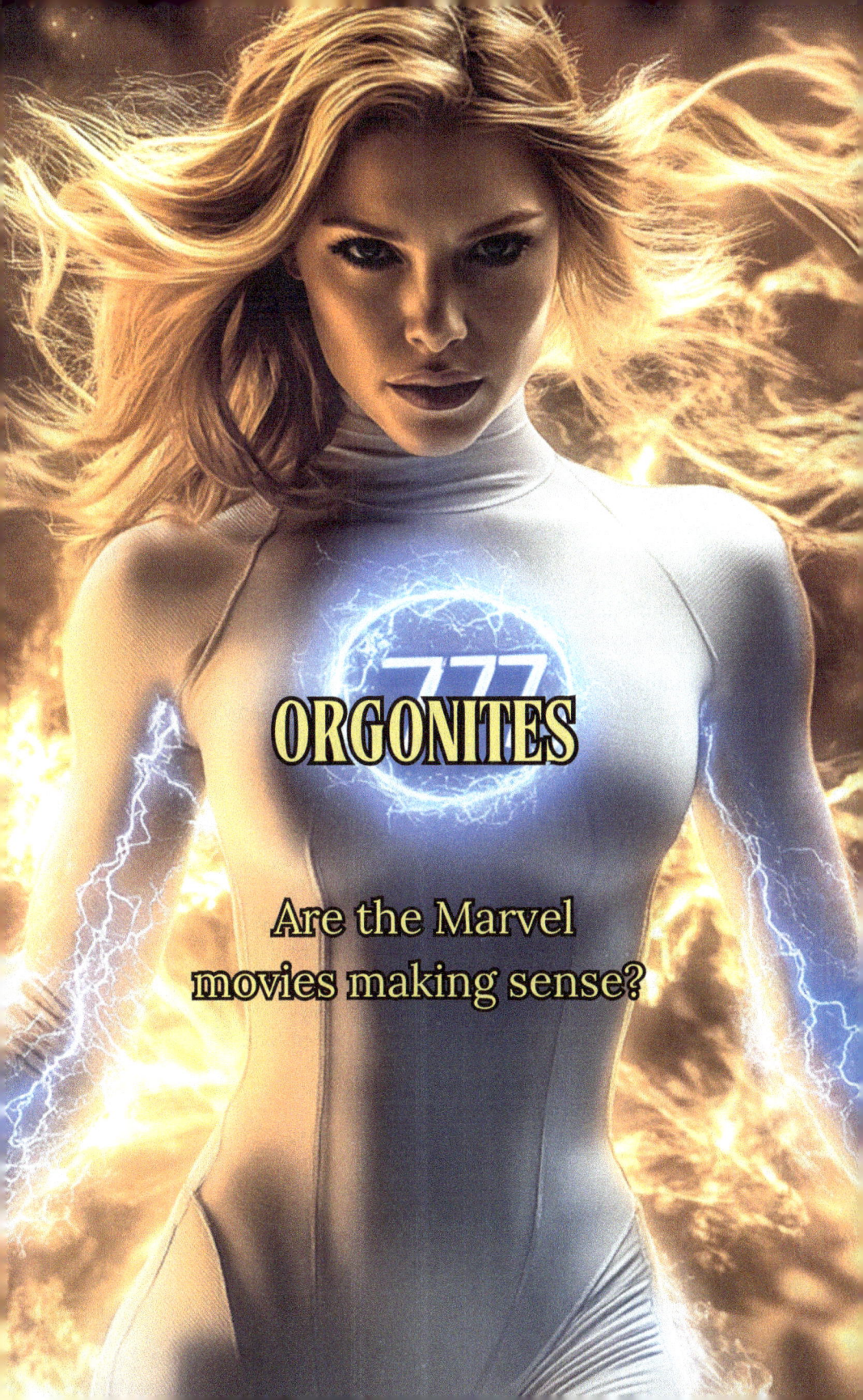

Superhero Insight: Wilhelm Reich and Orgonite Technology

Discovering Orgone Energy
Wilhelm Reich, an Austrian psychoanalyst, unveiled the concept of orgone energy in the 1930s. He believed this universal life force was present in all living matter.

Innovative Devices
To harness and study this energy, Reich created devices like:
- **Orgone Accumulator**: A box lined with layers of organic and metallic materials, claimed to improve health by increasing life energy flow.
- **Cloudbuster**: A device designed to manipulate orgone energy to produce rain.

Facing Controversy
Reich's groundbreaking ideas met skepticism and legal challenges. In the 1950s, the FDA accused him of making false claims about orgone energy and his devices. An injunction led to the destruction of his accumulators and related materials.

Imprisonment and Legacy
Reich was arrested for violating the injunction and sentenced to two years in prison. Tragically, he died in prison on November 3, 1957, under mysterious circumstances. Despite the controversy, his work continues to influence body psychotherapy and energy healing.

How Does It Work?
- Orgonite works by balancing and harmonizing the energy around you.
- The organic resin attracts positive orgone energy, while the inorganic metals disperse it, effectively neutralizing negative energy and electromagnetic pollution (EMFs).

When infused with crystals, orgonite becomes a powerful healing tool.

Crystals in Orgonite - EXAMPLES
Different crystals can enhance orgonite's effects:
- Quartz: Amplifies energy flow and enhances clarity.
- Amethyst: Promotes calmness and spiritual growth.
- Rose Quartz: Encourages love and emotional healing.
- Black Tourmaline: Provides grounding and protection against negativity.
- Citrine: Attracts abundance and positivity.

My experience with these OG's is the infused crystals create piezoelectric effects by transforming negative energy into harmonic and balanced energy.

I use these for sick animals, in my garden and for transplants. I've made many of these. I can tell you it is rather expensive to make them as you need to buy the crystals, metals (organic metals work best), and resin.

- I make these and they are available from the Alchemists in OH.
    - They are for sale on my "GROUNDCREW" TikTok shop @guardian_commander (https://www.tiktok.com/@guardian_commander) or you can email my editor at CML5@YAHOO.COM for a brochure.
    - Each one is hand-crafted and is self-charging and authentic. Each and every one of them is amazing and they all EXCEED my expectations!

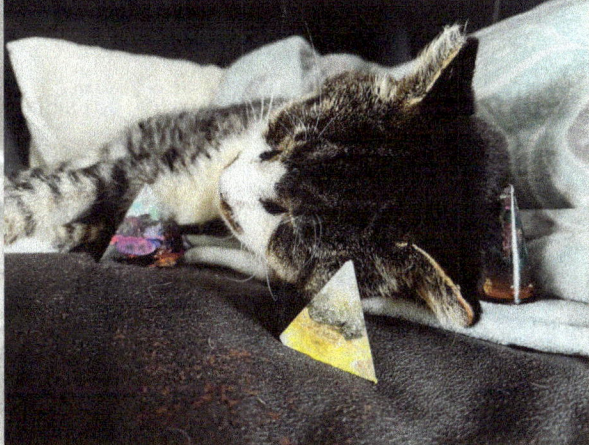

A rescue stray showed up with a hole in his chest. He required surgery. Here he is in rehab in my house.

I'm convinced he's a FLERKEN. He had a full recovery and is an indoor/outdoor LYRAN. We call him BIG BOY.

A Flerken is a fascinating alien species from the Marvel Universe! They look like ordinary Earth cats but possess extraordinary abilities. Look it up!!

Benefits of Orgonite:
- **EMF Protection**: Shields against harmful electromagnetic frequencies.
- **Energy Balancing**: Harmonizes your energy field.

Environmental Purification: Cleanses negativity from your surroundings.

Improved Well-being: Enhances your physical, mental, and spiritual health.

Orgonites made properly can be POWERFUL SMALL PORTABLE ENERGY HEALING CONVERTERS VITAL to our well-being. All living beings are attracted to them.

Embrace the revolutionary ideas of Wilhelm Reich and explore the potential of orgone energy to unlock your superhero potential!

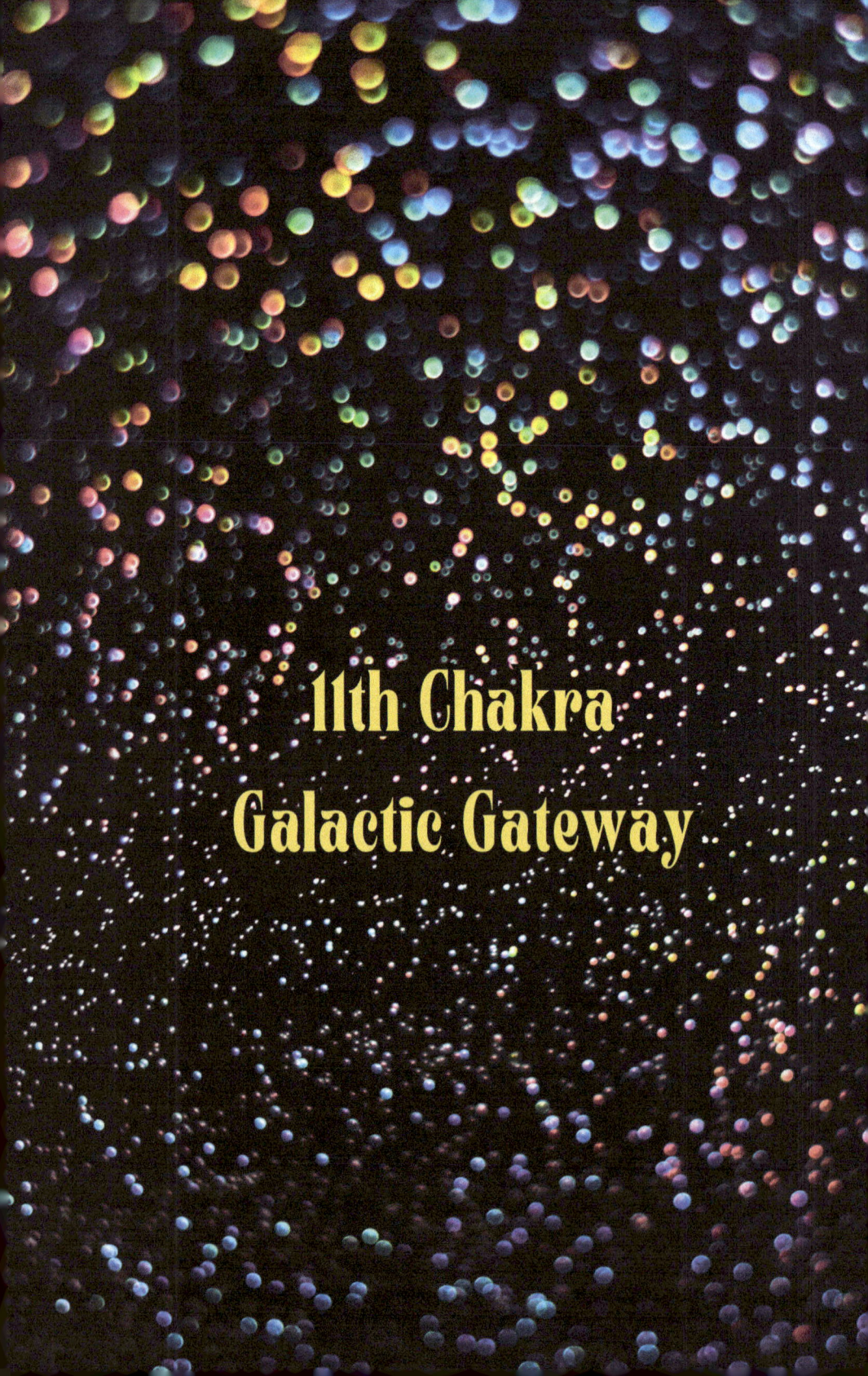

11th Chakra
The Galactic Gateway

Location: Above the 10th Chakra.
Color: The Galactic Chakra is silver / black, located approximately 18" above the Crown Chakra.

Function: Opens the gateway to galactic consciousness. *It's like stepping through a cosmic portal to join your interstellar superhero team!*

Superhero Insight: Cosmic Ascension Stages

Merging Sun and Moon
- The Sun's (Sol) light merges with the Moon's (Luna) reflections, uniting to create a powerful superhero mindset.

Dark Mother Transformed
- The 11th Chakra, representing the Dark Universal Mother, transforms through Solar Light into the radiant Solar Feminine Principle, like a superhero reborn.

Divine Union
- The union of Divine Fire (Mother) and Water (Father) creates Azoth, a magical essence that births the Universal Cosmic Egg.
- This Egg manifests the 12D Ray of Cosmic Christ-Sophianic Consciousness, empowering your superhero abilities.

Lightbody Activation
- The 12D Ray integrates into your Lightbody, transforming you into a Kunda-Ray Diamond Sun superhero.
- The 11th Chakra merges with the 8th, igniting your body with Emerald Green and Aquamarine colors, creating the Cosmic Holy Parent light body.

Unified Chakras
- Your chakras merge into a Unified Column, symbolizing unity and strength.

Epic 11D Timelines
- The 11th dimension is the battlefield for cosmic conflicts. These ancient battles reconnect to our cellular memory, manifesting for resolution.
- The 11D Stargate at Stonehenge, UK, serves as the gateway to these epic timelines.

Hieros Gamos Union

Superhero Insight: Hieros Gamos Union

- Hieros Gamos is the sacred union of divine masculine and feminine energies. It's important to balance these energies.
- It's like the ultimate superhero team-up within you, where these powerful forces combine to create balance, harmony, and higher consciousness.
- Think of it as a magical fusion of energy that transforms you into a more complete and powerful being, integrating both aspects of your inner self.
- This sacred union enhances your spiritual journey and amplifies your inner strength.

The sacred union of Hieros Gamos involves

- **Stage 1**: Solar Egg (10D) – Integrates Solar Light, powering up your superhero spirit.
- **Stage 2**: Lunar Egg (11D) – Integrates Moon's wisdom, balancing your hero's journey.
- **Stage 3**: Cosmic Egg (12D) –male & female within TWIN FLAME. Combines Solar and Lunar Light, embodying the ultimate Cosmic Christos Avatar, completing your superhero transformation.

Superhero Insight:

Activating the Hieros Gamos union, the sacred merging of divine masculine and feminine energies, involves these key steps:

- **Inner Balance**
    - Foster balance between your masculine and feminine energies. Embrace qualities like strength and compassion, action and reflection, logic and intuition.
- **Meditation and Mindfulness**
    - Practice regular meditation and mindfulness to connect deeply with your inner self. Focus on balancing your energies and visualizing their harmonious union.
- **Heart-Centered Living**
    - Live from your heart, embracing love, empathy, and kindness. This nurtures the compassionate and nurturing aspects of your being.
    - Address and heal past traumas that may block your inner balance. Engage in practices like inner child healing, energy healing, or self-reflection to release emotional baggage.
- **Spiritual Practices**
    - Incorporate spiritual practices that resonate with you, such as yoga, chakra balancing, working with sacred symbols.
    - I use ORGONITE CHAKRAS . See Section on Orgonites, pages 120-124, included in this book. These practices help align your energies.

- **Embrace Unity**
  - Recognize and honor the interconnectedness of all things.
  - Embrace unity and strive to see the divine in yourself and others.

- **Intention and Affirmation**
  - Set clear intentions and affirmations for union.
  - Declare your willingness to integrate and balance your energies, inviting the sacred union within.

Unlock your superhero potential, navigate these cosmic ascension stages, and achieve higher consciousness!

Superhero Insight: Signs of Balance and Higher Chakra Activation

Operating from your higher chakras and having balanced energies show through several signs:

- **Inner Peace and Calm**
  - You feel a deep sense of inner peace and calm, even in challenging situations. Stress and anxiety no longer dominate your thoughts.

- **Compassion and Empathy**
  - You naturally exhibit compassion and empathy towards others. Understanding and kindness flow effortlessly from you.

- **Intuitive Guidance**
  - Your intuition is strong and reliable. You often receive clear insights and guidance from within, helping you make wise decisions.

- **Clear Communication**
  - Your communication is clear and authentic. You express yourself truthfully and listen with an open heart, fostering deep connections.

- **Spiritual Connection**
  - You feel a strong connection to your higher self, the universe, and a sense of unity with all beings. Spiritual practices bring you profound joy and fulfillment.

- **Creative Flow**
  - Creativity flows effortlessly. You are inspired and find joy in creative pursuits, expressing your unique talents.

- **Emotional Stability**
  - Emotions are balanced and stable. You handle life's ups and downs with grace, maintaining a positive outlook.

- **Physical Vitality**
  - Your physical health and energy levels are vibrant. You feel strong, energized, and in tune with your body's needs.

- **Presence and Mindfulness**
  - You live in the present moment, fully aware and engaged. Mindfulness becomes a natural part of your daily life.

- **Aligned Purpose**
    - You have a clear sense of purpose and direction. Your actions align with your higher goals and values, bringing a sense of fulfillment and meaning.

Recognize these signs and continue nurturing your superhero potential by maintaining balance and operating from your higher chakras!

Earth's Natural Stargates

The Planetary Stargate System are the Earth's connection points or Portals into the Galactic and Universal Stargate Systems. They were once sealed off and closed, but now these Stargates are progressively opening during the Ascension Cycle.

Earth's Natural Stargates	
11D Stargate Vale of Pewsey	Amesbury, Wiltshire, UK (Stonehenge) 51.1679° N, 1.763° W
11D Inner gate Ireland's Eye	Irish Sea 53.404608° N, 6.063344° W
11D Inner gate St. Ives Bay	Cornwall, UK 50.211° N, 5.48° W (Grual-Grail Point)

* Refer to the Galactic Zodiac Section for additional stargates.

The 11th Galactic Orgonite Chakra (shimmering silver and black): is located approximately 18 inches above the Crown Chakra in the 4th Harmonic Universe.

At this spiritual ascension level, the angelic human Lightbody integrates all lower forms and identities, with the 11th Chakra descending into the throat, replacing the 5th (Throat) Chakra.

Infused with Cosmic Elements
These unique chakras are infused with:

- High-frequency crystals
- Grounding crystals
- Recharging elements
- Self-cleaning properties
- Organic metals
- This combination provides EMF protection and harmonizes radiation fields.

You can purchase these directly from the ALCHEMISTS (Ohio).

Email: CML5@YAHOO.COM for a brochure.

Sacred Sands from Stargates
The sands used in these chakras were collected from stargates around the world, including Giza, Israel, Jordan, and Bermuda by dedicated grid workers. Each orgonite is uniquely hand-crafted, ensuring no two are the same.

These orgonites are not needed to open your higher chakras. I just love working with crystals and found these to authentically align with my higher chakra opening.

I carry them in my pockets, place them under my pillow, and on my nightstand.

12th Chakra

12th Chakra
Earth Star

Location: Above the 11th Chakra.
Color: Pure white, embodying all colors.
Function: Merges you with universal oneness.
- It connects into the 12th dimension in the future timelines and is the 12D Ray of the Christ Mind.
- Invision yourself meditating in the heart of a supernova, finding peace and unity in the chaos of the universe.

Superhero Insight: Lightbody Interface

- **Planetary Interface -** Our Lightbody connects us to the planetary grid and its neural network system, such as the Planetary Logos. The Planetary Logos is the collective consciousness of Earth, like the brain of the planet, guiding its spiritual evolution.

12D Shielding

Superhero Insight: 12D Frequency Hubs
- Earth is being exposed to higher reality fields through concentrated energetic structures called "Frequency Hubs." These hubs create energetic portals at various locations, similar to crop circles.
- The 12D Frequency Hubs are placed on energetic vortices in concentric patterns, stabilizing the planet's grid and allowing accelerated frequency transmission to humans.

New Earth Experience
- These hubs introduce high-vibrating energies and allow access to life forms never before present. They support Lightworkers (Indigos and soul groups) on their Ascension mission and serve as Safe Zones.
- Soul Groups are assembling and recognizing each other to connect with the Frequency Hubs and activate cellular memory. The hubs facilitate the frequency needed for cellular activation in Indigos' emotional and cognitive centers.

Ascension Progression
- As we ascend spiritually and embody higher frequencies, our Lightbody channels these energies into the earth grid.

Supporting Evolution
- This connection helps Earth sustain higher frequencies, aiding the collective consciousness and the DNA patterns of all inhabitants, promoting evolutionary Ascension.

Superhero Insight: Meeting Soul Connections

Spiritual Ascension
- As we spiritually ascend and activate new dimensional frequencies in our light body, we often meet new beings who feel instantly familiar, like soul family or soul mates.

Dimensional Connections
- At each level of ascension, you connect with different beings, both in the inner planes and the physical world.
- These connections help you complete, heal, and activate each other.

Recognition and Activation
- These soul connections allow you to experience the joy of recognition with new or old spiritual friends.
- These beings or people couldn't enter your holographic field of perception until you held the specific frequency and light needed.

Superhero Insight: Safezones

Safezones explained:
- My farm is located in a safezone. It is an Ascending Hub area with high-frequency energy, fostering positive vibes and stability for the animals and everyone who visits it.

Positive Environment - Ascending Hub Area:
- The environment feels positive and lighter, making everyone feel more at ease.
- People in the area are kinder, often smiling and showing genuine compassion towards each other.
- The land is alive with abundant nature and animal spirits, adding to the serene and vibrant atmosphere.

Descending Hub Areas

Low-Frequency Symptoms
- Descending hub areas are plagued by crime, negativity, and destructive actions. The land feels lifeless and barren, and instability is seen in politics, economy, and social structures.
- For someone with a 12D Shield or Higher Sensory Perception, negativity is amplified and easily discerned.
- Those disconnected and miserable will resonate with the low energy due to their unresolved conflicts and suffering.

Synchronization of Frequency Hubs

- As more people experience the Bifurcation of Time, they attract others with similar frequencies, forming group consciousness and shared realities.
- These "reality bubbles" of belief systems will spread globally, creating synchronized areas of matching frequency.
- This phase synchronizes frequency hubs worldwide, either descending or ascending in vibrational quality.
- Do you live in an ascending or descending frequency hub?
- Why do you resonate with that HUB?

Embrace the power of synchronization and join forces with like-minded superheroes to elevate the planet's frequency!

Orgonite EARTH STAR 12th Chakra

For those of you who like **crystals** - these are the higher chakras in ORGONITE!!

These Earth Star Orgonites (12th Chakra) are infused with sands, high frequency crystals, grounding crystals, recharging, self-cleaning, and organic metals to bring EMF protection and to harmonize radiation fields. These are amazing! *I have many of these. I love crystals and the higher chakras are hard to find.*

The Earth Star is located 6 inches below your feet and holds hydroplasmic liquid light blueprint to your original angelic 12 DNA strands. This Chakra holds the KEY to your organic memories/future 12D timelines and your lightbody activation. Carry this orgonite with you or place in your pillow when you sleep. These fit nicely in your hand as well.

This special orgonite is infused with opalite, selenite, high frequency metals, rainbow moonstone, shungite, labradorite, and sand carrying the 432 hertz for Gaia.

I hand made these and they are one of kind and hand-infused (all in one)! Available by email CML5@yahoo.com. These are affordable, self-charging and high frequency organic metals and crystals.

13th Chakra
The Earth Core Chakra

Location: Beneath your feet, grounding you to Earth.
Color: Aquarmarine
Function: Anchors you to the planet's core energy.
Think of yourself stomping your foot and feeling the Earth's fiery strength coursing through you, ready to defend it!

Superhero Insight: Activating the Earth Core Chakra

Earth Core Chakra
- The Earth Core Chakra is Aquamarine and connects to the Universal Mother Arc at the base of the 12D Shield, located 12 inches below your feet and extending into the earth core.

Igniting the 12D Shield
- First, build and ignite the 12D Shield with the 12D Ray.
- This prepares the Mother Arc to ignite within the earth and your personal Lightbody shield.
- This is the real Blue Ray activation of Mother Arc.

Chakra Activation
- This activation ignites Mother's Blue Ray, granting access to Mother Arc Portals (Arc Gates) within the earth.
- It then moves into the Transharmonic Gates or 13th Pillar, spinning Aqua Portals in higher dimensions for safe passage through the Universal Core and into Andromeda or other Universal Gates.

Hieros Gamos Integration
- In the third stage of Hieros Gamos sacred marriage integration, the Aqua Ray ignites in the 13th Chakra, ascends up the unified chakra column, merges with the 3rd and 4th Chakras, and resides in the still point of the chest.
- This embodies the Holy Mother of God principle.

Running Aqua Ray Fields
- Upon embodying the Holy Mother Arc, which ignites the Inner Holy Spirit in our Diamond Heart, you can run Aqua Ray fields and direct them on the earth plane.

Superhero Insight: Founder Aqua Blue Ray
Threefold Founder Flame
- To connect with the Founder Aqua Blue Ray and reclaim the Mother of God principle for the planet and humanity, we connect to the Aqua Blue Ray of Mother Arc.

History of the Blue Ray
- Previously, the Blue Ray was under the control of the Melchizedek hosting our planet. Since the Sumerian-Egypt Invasion, the Mother Arc Aqua Blue Ray was absent from the earth core, leading to the loss of the Mother of God and female Christ Sophianic Body principle.

Ascension Cycle
- The Ascension Cycle is about reclaiming the Christ and Mother principles for the planet. During this cycle, the fragmented Blue Ray was used by the Melchizedek and Family of Michael forces.

Reignition of Mother Arc
- In 2009, Mother Arc was reignited in the earth core and in many Mother Arc Hub Gates on the Earth's surface. This event restored access to the Mother of God, the Holder of the Founder Aqua Blue Ray, and opened the 13th Gate into the Neutron Window. This connection links us to the Aurora and Krystal Star.

Andromeda Core
- The Aquaferion races were lines that were a part of the original Krystal Star human race lines that became extinct in this Universal Time Matrix after the Electric Wars.
- When the Mother Arc was ignited in the earth core, the inner gates which connect to Andromeda were opened through the Crystal Core of the earth.
- The protectors of the crystal core are of these krystic races called Aquaferions or Aquari lines. The Aquaferion Councils from Andromeda started to be able to be in contact with the Indigo race lines approximately early 2008.
- Many of us are genetically related to the Aquaferion races which have a direct genetic relationship to Christ lineages.
- Some of us will undergo genetic rehabilitation through our Aquaferion DNA links which connect us to the future planet in Andromeda Galaxy.
- For some of us this is our future ascended Christos body in the next incarnation.

Reminder: Only take what resonates with you. Everyone is at their own level of integration and that is perfectly okay.

Superhero Insight: Mother Arc Hubs
Mother Arc Hubs

Earth Core Chakra:
- The Earth Core Chakra is Aquamarine and connects to the Universal Mother Arc at the base of the 12D shield, 12 inches below your feet and extending into the earth core.
- This Aqua Ray activation of Mother Arc returns the Blue Ray to the Mother. Connecting with the Threefold Founder Flame under Aqua Blue Ray reclaims the Mother of God principle for the planet and humanity.

Mother Principle:
- By uniting with our Mother Principle, the Mother Arc 13th Pillar and 13th Aqua Ray, we are led into the Ascended Master fields of the Rainbow Rays and the Aurora time continuum, connecting to the liquid light of Pale Aqua Rays from the Aqualine Sun.

Mother Arc Amplifier \ Mother's Aquamarine Chalice:
- The Mother Arc Amplifier is an Andromedan Amplifier (Talisman). It represents the Mother Principle, Eternal Holy Spirit, the Staff of Power, and the Aquamarine Chalice.

Mother Arc Essence:
- Mother Arc embodies the Aurora Ether, Zero Point merged with the Aquamarine Founder Ray.
- It is the Staff frequency and architecture of the Arc of the Covenant, a living consciousness portal system on this planet.

Even my horses like them! This is the Earth Core Orgonite Chakra with one of my draft horses inspecting it.

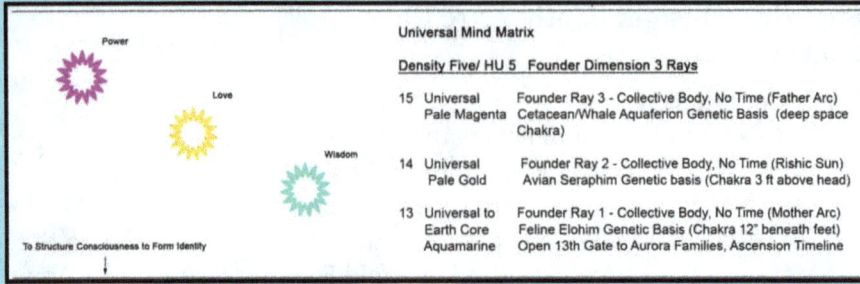

** Special thanks to Lisa Renee with EnergeticSynthesis.com

Superhero Insight: What is the Mother Arc?

Mother Arc Portal

- **13th Pillar, 13th Gateway:** Functions with the Transharmonic Gates.
- **Aquamarine Ray Energy:** Guardians call this aspect of Mother's energy a new quality of magnetic force powering up in our Earth Core.
- **Aqua Ray Frequency:** This energy comes from the earth core's newly reconnected 9D Merkabic structure, flooding the planetary body with Aqua Ray frequency.
- **Reconnecting with Mother Arc:** We've broken through the mind-controlled frequency fence and reconnected with the Aqua Ray frequency and the braided plasma fields of the Aqualine Sun.
- **Override Pillar Gates:** These gates reconnect us with the original parent frequency, healing our inner spirit and Lightbody.

Mother Arc Stargate Locations
1 Adare, Ireland
2 Stonehenge, England
3 Seattle, Wash, US
4 Manhattan Island, US
5 Bali, South Pacific
6 Uluru (Ayers Rock), Australia
7 Phoenix, Arizona US
8 Atlantic Ocean, SW of Bermuda (64.9W, 32.1N)
9 Antarctica (13W, 88S)
10 Baghdad, Iraq
11 Newgrange Ireland
12 Cornwall, UK

14th Chakra: The Universal Sun Chakra

Location: This amazing chakra hovers about 3 feet above your head, connecting you to the Universal Sun with the Founders' Pale Gold Ray.
Color: Golden, like a brilliant pale sunrise.
Function: Connects you to the energy of the universal sun.

Imagine recharging your superhero powers directly from a cosmic sunrise.

The Golden Fleece Buffer

Top Lid of the 12D Shield
- This Chakra acts as the top lid of the 12D Shield, creating a powerful protective field called the Golden Fleece Buffer when activated.

Golden Fleece Buffer
- The Golden Fleece Buffer is an advanced protection shield, invisible to most of the Negative Alien Agenda (NAA).
- It combines the 14D Founder Gold Ray, 12D Ray, and 12D Shield, along with the 8th Chakra activation of the Monad.

Liquid Plasma Pillar
- This chakra, when activated with the 8th layer of the higher heart complex in the Monadic body, expands to form the Golden Fleece Buffer from the solar plexus.
- This specialized protection shield in the Monadic body layer allows safe passage through the Arc Zone and keeps consciousness invisible to the NAA fallen timekeepers during transharmonic field navigation.

Arc of the Covenant Activation
- The activation of the Arc of the Covenant gate system on Earth also activates the Golden Fleece Buffer.
- This shield is designed to protect our physical bodies from severe anti-Christ reversal currents set in motion by retaliating NAA forces.

Superhero Insight: Paliadorians and Arc Technology

Paliadorian Agreement
- After the Fall of Tara, advanced Krystic races from the God Worlds, known as the Paliadorians, agreed to help Earth and humanity.
- They introduced the advanced technology of the Ancient Builder Races, including the Arc of the Covenant and its Stargate network.

Arc of the Covenant
- The Arc of the Covenant is a portal bridge spanning multiple dimensions and time-space locations between Earth and Andromeda.
- It acts as a host matrix, designed for genetic rehabilitation to reset the divine blueprint for healing the soul, monad, and Avatar crystal body in the original angelic human template.

Paliadorian Activations
- Ongoing Paliadorian Activations transmit instruction sets to those on the Christos mission, allowing the assembly of the Arc of the Covenant code sets within our lightbody.
- Nothing on earth is safer than being in one's own 12D Shield and activated Lightbody.
- We hold the instruction set for future embodiment of the Arc codes, assembling the field as a group from the 13th Pillar Essene spiritual lineages with the Christos-Sophia rainbow plasma shield.

Host Matrix Transplant
- Together, we have the potential to enact the Host Matrix Transplant for the entire planet, reclaiming all lines within the 12 Essene Tribes.
- This Host matrix template acts as a krystal bridge, dissolving artificial timelines and AI machinery, collapsing the NAA architecture supporting anti-Christ patriarchal systems.

14th Chakra Orgonite
- I created this 14th Chakra Orgonite.
- It is infused with all organic crystals and is amazing.
- I truly resonate with crystals and know their power.
- These are like crystals on steroids!!

Superhero Insight: Fifth Harmonic Universe

Stations of Identity
- In the Fifth Harmonic Universe, consciousness bodies exist throughout the densities as aspects of the higher self and Lightbody.
- These are called the Stations of Identity.

Three Layers of the Rishi Matrix
- In the 13D-14D-15D of the Fifth Harmonic Universe, you'll find the Three Layers of the Rishi Matrix, also known as the Threefold Founder Flame or GSF Flame.
- These collective consciousness bodies are connected to Earth's future timelines and Lightbody, interfacing with human consciousness across all densities.

Pre-Matter Zone
- In the Fifth Harmonic Universe, there are no matter forms, no planetary body, or human forms.
- This pre-matter zone is where consciousness exists without manifesting into matter.

Trinity of the Godhead
- The three primal light and sound fields in this universe express the rays of Mother Arc, Father Arc, and Golden Ray Sun of Christos.
- These rays form the trinity of the Godhead, from which all biological forms are created across all Harmonic Universes.

Superhero Insight: The Gold Order

Second Emanation of Primal Sound Field
- The Gold Order is the second emanation of the Primal Sound Field, representing the second individuation of the God Source.
- It is part of the Cosmic Trinity, also known as the Threefold Founder Flame.

Light Manifestation of the Gold Order
- The Gold Order manifests as the Gold Ray orders of Seraphim, Cerez Avian bird people, and Aeithan lines.
- These are the Solar Rishi who incarnated in the fourth harmonic universe on Lyra-Vega through the 10th Universal Stargate.

Superhero Insight: Sound Tones
Gold Order Visuals
- The Gold Order is associated with bright light golden halos, often accompanied by white halos glowing with gold and silver showers. There can be faint colors mixed in, creating a radiant visual effect.

Seraphei Lineages
- The Seraphei lineages are highly responsive to visual stimuli, connecting deeply with these luminous golden halos.

Superhero Insight: Royal Houses of Lyra
Royal Houses
- The Trinity of the Emerald Order, Gold Order, and Amethyst Order incarnated in the fourth Harmonic Universe within the Lyran Matrix are known as the Royal Houses.

Superhero Insight: 10D Fallen Draconian Rehabilitation
Rehabilitation Mission
- Due to the human Tribal Shield affiliation and genetic ties to the 10th Stargate and Golden Eagle Grid, many of the Gold Order have been appointed to rehabilitate and transit the Draconian race lines, overriding their Negative Alien Agenda (NAA) related timelines.

Dragon Moth Lines & GOLD Order
- The fallen 10D lines from Vega became the Dragon Moth lines, resulting from the hybridization between the Gold Order Seraphim and fallen Draconian lines.

Connecting to the Gold Ray
- To reclaim our Christos-Sophia principle for the planet and humanity, we connect to the Gold Ray of Rishic Suns.
- This Gold Ray was previously controlled by the distorted Golden Eagle Grid and damaged by Fallen Angelics.

Healing Efforts
- Since the Luciferian Rebellion, the Golden Eagle Grid and Gold Ray suffered distortion. Guardians are working to heal this damage to the Seraphim-Avian consciousness through the Shield of Solomon, aiming to restore the planet's masculine principle and Rod function.

Morphogenetic Chakras
- In higher spiritual development, starting with Monadic Integration, Morphogenetic Chakras (8-15) merge into a Unified Column. This gender unification of male and female principle chakras creates a unified consciousness column.

Superhero Insight: RA Center

RA Center in Krystallah Body
- In an activated lightbody, the Solar Plexus reconfigures into a Golden Solar Gate energy vortex called the RA Center.
- This golden orb body, stemming from the 14th Chakra, houses the conscious identity.

Higher Embodiment
- During higher embodiment activation, the 1D and 2D frequency layers dissolve, leaving a Solar Sacrum above the navel, forming the RA Center. With Diamond Sun Body Activation, male-female spirals merge into a large light orb around the body, creating unified energy spheres along the central column.

Platinum Crystals and Sun Discs
- Connected to the Sun Disc Network, Platinum Crystals in Earth balance feminine-masculine principles and heal anti-life reversal currents.
- This reconfigures the solar plexus into the Golden Solar Gate energy vortex, the RA Center.

Inner Solar Temple
- The Solar Logos, or Solar King, illuminates our inner Sun Temple within the solar plexus.
- It provides warmth, growth, and protection, helping build our inner spiritual light.
- The Solar King amplifies strength and endurance, especially during trauma, guiding us to rebuild our inner Sun Temple and connect with Earth's Sun Temples.

Superhero Insight: Aton Solar Disk
- The Aton Solar Disk becomes an embodied shield within the ascending Starseeded and human Lightbody, integrating into the solar sacrum and RA Center of the Krystallah Double Diamond Sun DNA Template during the Ascension Cycle.

Restoring the Solar Sacrum
- As part of restoring the Solar Sacrum in the gender center, the Aton Solar Disk activates into the 10-11-12D Solar Logos base shield beneath the feet.
- This aligns with the 10D Solar Star above the head, repatterning into the higher crown center.

Crown Shift
- This transformation shifts the crown into the organic North Star, leading home back to the God Worlds.

Superhero Insight: Double Diamond Sun Body

24D Oraphim Krystal Star Template
- The Double Diamond Sun Body is the 24D Oraphim Krystal Star template from the Seven Higher Heavens in Andromeda.
- Mother and Father have returned their 24D Double Diamond Sun Oraphim to this Universe, bringing the liquid Christos light to our planet.

Starseeds and Indigos' Mission
- Starseeds and Indigos have come to Earth during the Ascension cycle to help build this "house" and embody the eternal Christos plasma light.
- This is a powerful physical body healer, and when in use with the 12D Shield will start to automatically build in your Lightbody aura, as it is the organic matrix of light body.
- This is the amplifier for physical pain, sickness or rehabilitation of the "vehicles". Charging objects for children or pets with this frequency, is suggested, when feeling ill or during sleep time. Christos embodies his parents, loving compassion, and lives in perfect peace and harmony with all things.

Embodied Unity
- Christos embodies loving compassion, living in harmony with all things. This Tetramorphic Symbol represents a Perfected Eternal Human Being, male and female, wearing an Aurora Crown, and emanating a rainbow Aurora Krystal **Shield.**

Krystallah Merkaba Fields
- The Krystallah merkaba fields, made up of the Universal Androgynous Merkaba fields of Christos-Sophia, are crucial for building the Ascension Vehicle.
- These fields, generated from the Holy Mother Arc in the 13th Gateway, align the male and female energies for sacred union, guiding the creation of merkaba fields.

Double Diamond Sun DNA
24 Strand

See EnergeticSynthesis.Com

Diamond Sun 12 Strand DNA
- When the Crystal Body light and sound layers unify into one body, this stage of Lightbody development opens up the possibility to generate different sound light emanations into liquid light Plasma Waves.
- This is the generation of hierogamic crystalline blueprints in the crystal body that further activate the Crystal Gene in the Silicate Matrix which then catalyzes a range of Bio-Spiritual Plasmas.

12 Strand DNA
- All 12 genetic components of the 12 Tribes hold one strand of DNA code for reassembling the Crystal Gene for the Diamond Sun body or Silicate Matrix, that is key coded to activate the 12 layers of the planetary stargate system.
- This provides the means to contact our higher Stations of Identity as spiritual bodies, and to connect with the conscious living light and sound frequencies in the holographic matrix.
- The instruction sets to rebuild and reassemble the 12 Strand DNA pattern, are held in the genetic keys found in the Cosmic Kryst-Krystallah blueprint which makes up the 12 Tree Grid manifestation template.

Mothers Missing Chromosomes
- Most of our genes are stored in our chromosomes, which sit in each cell's headquarters or the nucleus.
- We also have some genes in small structures in the cell called Mitochondria, which hold an active potential for igniting the Crystal Gene.

Crystal Gene Gender Merge
- It is the spiritual mission of recently assigned Rod and Staff couplings to template the prototype blueprint to achieve spiritual marriage or Hieros Gamos, and work to bring this into a physically manifested accomplishment.
- This is happening at various octave levels (relationship assignments, Soul, Monad and Avatar Christos-Sophia dimensional levels) to eventually achieve a complete re-encryption of the masculine rod function to the spinning 12:12 electron pattern, that merges perfectly into the female monadic core, a 13:13 field. This is a template prototype that is called the KRYST HALA or the Krystallah Pattern, which is the Crystal Gene Gender Merge between genetic equals.

Keepers of Blue and Violet Flame
- The Keepers of the Blue Flame and Violet Flame hold the genetic configuration of the Crystal Gene in their Mitochondria and this holds the entire 12 Strand DNA imprint.
- This is designed to help support the Paliadorians with the ongoing planetary grid repairs necessary for correcting fallen and artificial timelines and remaining on the Cosmic Father's divine plan for ongoing planetary Ascension.

15th Chakra
The Universal Father Chakra

Location: The highest point in the chakra system.
Color: Magenta symbolizing divine masculine energy.
Function: Links you to the universal father principle.

Picture receiving cosmic wisdom from a divine father figure, ready to guide you on your mission.

15th Chakra and Universal Father Ray
- The 15th Chakra connects to the Universal Father Ray, colored Pale Magenta, located in Deep Space beneath us and Earth.
- During Hieros Gamos sacred marriage integration, the Pale Magenta-Violet Ray ignites in the 12th Chakra, merging with the 1st Chakra and the Mother's Aqua Ray, bringing in Cosmic Monad waves (Emerald Green Ray).
- This embodies the Cosmic Holy Father of God principle.

Elevating Embodiment
- This process elevates the individual out of the 1D-2D-3D Chakra Wave Spectrum, protecting them from lower density energies and reversal polarity problems.

Founder Magenta Ray
- To connect with the Founder Magenta Ray and reclaim our Father of God principle, we connect to the Magenta Ray of Father Arc.
- This ray was previously distorted by the Planetary Logos invasion and the Moon Chain lineages promoting patriarchal domination.
- The Mother Arc has reclaimed the Holy Father's consciousness for Earth.

Fifth Harmonic Universe
- For humans, consciousness bodies exist throughout densities as aspects of the higher self and Lightbody, known as Stations of Identity.
- In the Fifth Harmonic Universe (13D-15D), the Three Layers of the Rishi matrix or Threefold Founder Flame exist.

Pre-Matter Zone
- In the Fifth Harmonic Universe, consciousness exists without manifesting into matter forms. The three primal light and sound fields express the rays of Mother Arc, Father Arc, and Golden Ray Sun of Christos, forming the trinity of the Godhead, creating all biological forms in all Harmonic Universes.

Superhero Insight: Cosmic Spiritual Sun and Transformation

Cosmic Spiritual Sun
- The Sun hides an etheric planetary orb, leading to the Cosmic Spiritual Sun or Sun Disc Network.
- This holds the first principle of the Holy Father's Eternal Light, the highest expression of The Solar King or Cosmic Christos Consciousness.

Father Arc and Mother Arc
- The Cosmic Holy Father principle, the Father Arc, is the source of the Cosmic Spiritual Sun. The Mother Arc is awakening the Holy Father Arc, bringing back the Cosmic Solar Masculine Christos principle through the Seven Sacred Suns (KA RA YA SA TA AA LA).

Alteration and Rehabilitation
- This new solar activity changes masculine archetypes, rehabilitating the 7D Violet Ray and correcting distortions like the Crucifixion Implants. This impacts the elemental particles of matter, making them less dense and dismantling the False Father masculine archetypes of Mind Control.

Return of the Solar King
- The planetary mind is to be replaced with the Christos mind, guided by the return of the Solar King, or Triple Solar Masculine Christ. This marks the return of the Holy Father's Rod architecture.

Awakening Holy Father
- The awakening Holy Father brings benevolent masculine forces. Ending the Tyrant's rule requires personal spiritual responsibility to break free from victim patterns.

Cosmic Monad of Father God
- The Cosmic Monad of Father God, or Father Arc, sends liquid plasma waves of the Cosmic Christos to activate or return the Permanent Seed Atom through plasma Lightbody and Emerald Crystal Heart activations. The merged Emerald Ray (Cosmic Holy Father and Mother) symbolizes the Return of Emerald Order, restoring energetic balance.

Permanent Seed Atom
- Located in the Higher Heart Chakra (8th Chakra), the Permanent Seed Atom holds all consciousness memory in the Universe.
- If damaged, it will be repaired and returned to its rightful owner, fostering spiritual growth and truth. The Higher Heart Center is called the Crystal Lotus Heart.

Superhero Insight: Healing the Father Archetype
Cultivating Virtues and Ethics
- The Cosmic Holy Father principle helps us address base issues, cultivating virtues and ethical principles to strengthen our spiritual roots.
- As we feel safer with God, we build trust in the father principle within ourselves, knowing we are protected and free from fear-based karma. This process heals unconscious root issues in our personal Tree of Life.

Grounded Masculine Principle
- Being in right relationship with the masculine principle means feeling grounded, stable, and secure with a strong inner core.
- This inner security isn't dependent on external circumstances.

Humanity's Progress
- Humanity can't evolve spiritually until the Father principle is healed and integrated.
- We're addressing root blockages caused by the False King of Tyranny. We must distinguish between the external False Father archetype and the internal Cosmic Holy Father, the essence of Christos Compassionate Witnessing.

Father Paradox
- Recognizing the "father paradox" helps us understand the foundational beliefs and frequencies in our spiritual foundation, working through inner, outer, and in-between worlds.

Superhero Insight: Finding Base Security with Father
Strong Base, Strong Father
- To find base security and inner stability, we must stop basing our self-esteem on outer circumstances.
- Our task is to free ourselves from being bullied, intimidated, or threatened, and to build trust in the Cosmic Holy Father within ourselves.
- This relationship with God is our true security.

Identifying Fear
- Identify what stimulates fear and victimhood and stop giving it power. Leave behind false beliefs of security, such as money, houses, or careers.
- True security comes from within, not external factors.

Overcoming False Security
- Using external items for security is a delusion of power designed to fail.
- This breaks self-esteem through betrayals of trust, creating codependence and frailty.
- Many are learning this painful lesson during this cycle.

Superhero Insight: Discern False Father from Real
Identifying False vs. Real Father Archetypes
- It's crucial to distinguish between the False Father, promoted by the NAA through the False King of Tyranny, and the authentic compassion of the Holy Father Arc to achieve true security, stability, and grounded spirituality.

Using a Chart for Balance
- A helpful chart can identify fear thought forms and negative archetypes from the False King of Tyranny.
- Intend and ask Holy Father Arc to balance these with positive thought forms, leading to unified patterns of balance in sacred marriage.

Tree of Life and Root Chakra
Grounding Ray Sacred Marriage: Merging with 15D Father and 7D Mother.
- **Balancing Archetype**: Earth Mother and Compassionate Father unite, creating a nurturing aspect.
- **Negative Archetypes:**
    - Blocked Root Chakra (Victim)
    - Too Open Root Chakra (Bully)
- **Tri-Wave Unified Pattern:** Harmony with self and others, stable, secure, and grounded.
- **Fear Thoughtforms - Negative Polarity:** Survival fears, poverty, unsafe, disease, entitled, disassociated, disconnection with material world.
- **Love Thoughtforms - Positive Polarity:** Safety, gratitude, abundance, ease, connection with spirit and material world.

1D Unconscious Pain/Separation - Four Main Areas of Father Healing:
1. Abuse
2. Trauma
3. Shock
4. Devastation

Horizontal Shields
- The horizontal shields represent the male principle of the mental body for all consciousness bodies.
- The Father Arc and Solomon Shield help heal the False King of Tyranny male principle within the Root Chakra on Earth.

Dimensional Integration
- When the five shields based on dimensional triads are integrated into the consciousness and Lightbody layers, the higher spiritual Rod function of the lightbody is activated.
- This activation connects higher intelligence mental bodies to their respective dimensions, known as the Horizontal Triad Bodies.
  - REMEMBER hearing 3-6-9?

Superhero Insight: 3-6-9 Rod Repair

Kundalini Correction
- When the Kundalini current flows correctly in the 3-6-9 dimensions, it helps build the subharmonic strings and the Horizontal Triad Bodies.

Building Higher Masculine Principles
- This process starts to build higher Masculine principle mental bodies, merging them into their Trinitized Form.

Metatronic Repair
- Correcting male mental body patterns in these higher mind matrices also leads to Metatronic repair, a Nephilim 9D body correction.

Activating the Masculine Rod
- When the three harmonic triads are corrected, the Lightbody structure known as the Masculine Rod initiates and activates in the Lightbody.

Horizontal Shields

Male Principle of Mental Body
- Horizontal shields represent the male principle of the mental body for all consciousness bodies across timelines in the Harmonic Universes.

Integration and Activation
- When these five shields, built on dimensional triads, integrate into the consciousness and Lightbody, they activate the higher spiritual masculine Rod function.

Higher Intelligence Activation
- This sequence activates higher intelligence mental bodies, connecting them to their respective dimensions.

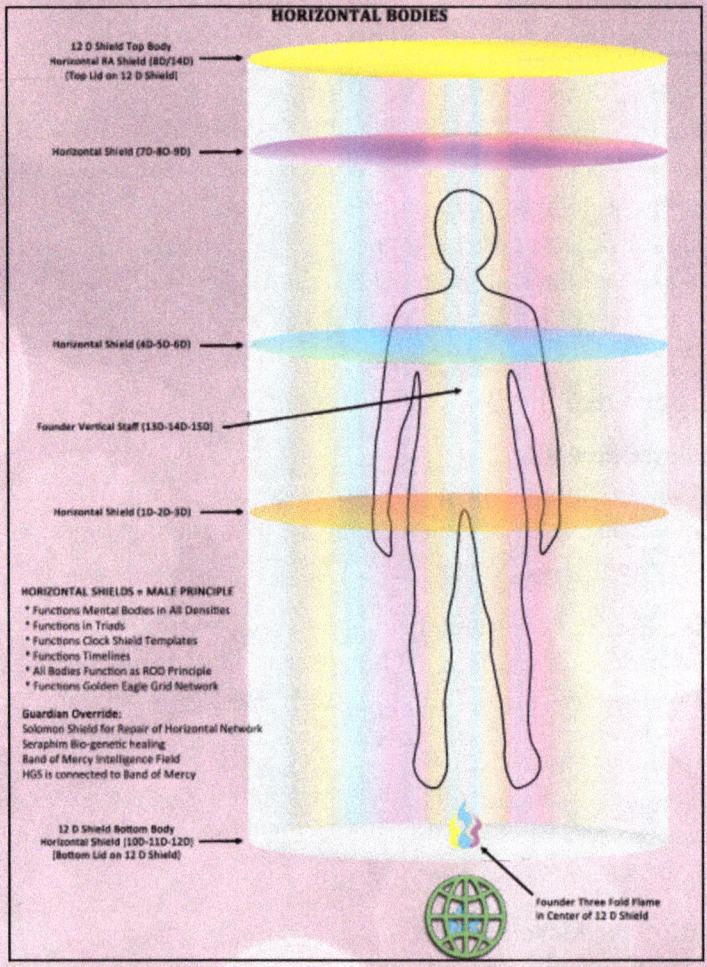

Photo from EnergeticSynthesis.Com

The 12D Shield configuration is what allows us to "phone home" to our family of Christ here in 3D matter Timelines, and this is why it's so important.

Superhero Insight: Harmonic Universes

Holographic Template
- When we incarnate on 3D Earth, we're imprinted with the holographic template of the Universal Tree of Life.
- This template includes five harmonic universe layers that direct our consciousness life stream through time and space.

Merkaba Field Spin Rates
- The five harmonic universe levels govern the spin rates of merkaba fields, which transmit electromagnetic currents based on the architectural laws and frequency characteristics of each system.

Planetary Cycles
- The spin rate of planetary merkaba fields influences the birth, evolution, and death cycles of the entire planetary species.

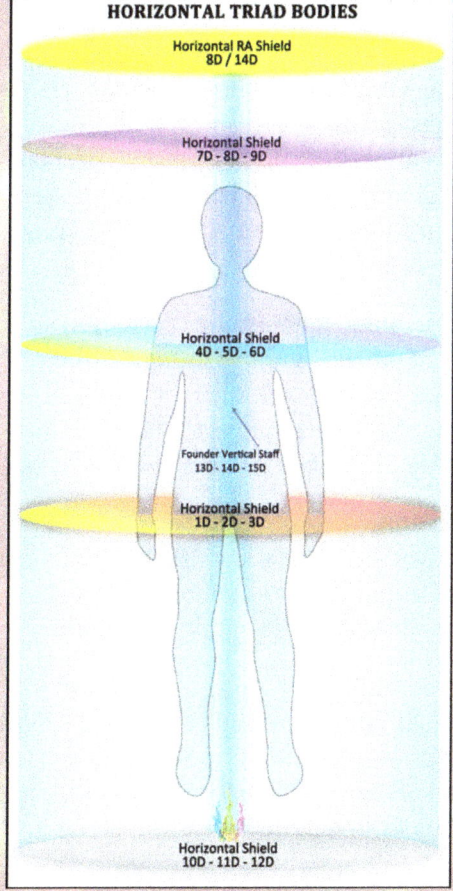

Photo from EnergeticSynthesis.Com

Superhero Insight: The Cosmic Spiritual Sun

Cosmic Spiritual Sun
- The Cosmic Spiritual Sun is the Spiritual Sun behind the Sun. It hides an etheric planet, an entrance to the Cosmic Spiritual Sun, which holds the first principle of the Father's Eternal Light, the Solar King in his Seven Sacred Suns.
- This Holy Father principle gives light to all things in the Universe, heralding the reappearance of the Cosmic Christos principle in our Solar System.

Seven Sacred Suns
- Previously beyond our reach due to a "ring-pass-not" around our Solar System, the Seven Sacred Suns are now returning to activity with the Earth and humanity.
- This release heralds the initiation of the planetary logos and the positive future evolution of collective humanity.

Solar Evolution
- Our visible Sun is undergoing a magnetic pole reversal, altering its Solar Ray transmissions.
- This change also affects the constellation Ursa Major and its seven main stars, merging with the Pleiades' Seven Sisters to form the Seven Sacred Suns in One, also known as the Aurora Sun.

Unified Solar Body
- The Seven Sacred Suns unite as one connected solar body to transmit Cosmic Spiritual Sun plasma waves, building the Christos Diamond Sun body in its Seven tones: KA RA YA SA TA AA LA.
- This collective is the Krystal Aegis, forming the Base Shield for the Eukachristic Body or Double Diamond Sun Body of the Oraphim.

Astrological Resolution
- This cosmic convergence clears miasmatic blueprints of karmic histories in stellar and cellular memory, dissolving "cosmic evil" and "cosmic rage" from multiple planetary histories.

Galactic Suns
- The Earth core has merged with parallel Earths in future timelines, weaving together with the Galactic Suns.
- This integration of Cosmic to Galactic Plasmic Sun Source, called the Aqualine Sun, is now more accessible in the Earth crust.

- Plasma infusions from the Galactic Suns and the Earth core have activated Mother Earth's Inner Sun frequencies, appearing as deep ultraviolet and bluish plasma light.
- This complete circuit of Galactic plasmic light transmissions, called the Aqualine Sun frequencies, is anchored into the Earth core and gradually merging with the Earth Sun.

Indigos, Starseeds, and the Oraphim
- These groups serve as conduits for transmitting ascending Aqualine Sun frequencies into the Earth, helping to anchor plasma infusions on the surface grid and repair damaged networks.

Superhero Insight: Generating Plasma Light

Plasma Light Potential
- The human body, made of atoms and ions, can generate Plasma through a biological ionization process.
- During the Ascension cycle, this process creates internal Plasma light, building the etheric Lightbody for higher consciousness.

Powering Up with Energy
- To generate internal Plasma light and build our Lightbody, we need abundant energy.
- By devoting personal energy and directing our consciousness toward spiritual development, we can conserve energy in the material world and expand our consciousness.

Building Energy with Meditation
- Meditation helps us build and conserve internal energy, achieving inner balance.
- This stops energy leaks and waste, increasing our direct connection to the God Source. With this connection, we can direct personal energy to spark the plasmic light.

Non-Polarized Base Shield
- The Seven Suns frequencies form a new base shield template, replacing the 3D Grounding Mechanism.
- This Base 360 degrees Grounding Shield allows entry into any timeline from within its center.
- It builds the Eukachristic Body for the Avatar Christos-Sophia consciousness, developing into the Krystallah eternal lightbody for the Omniversal Personal Christ on Earth and beyond.

Superhero Insight: Attuning to Plasma Light

Harnessing Plasma Light
Attune to the power of plasma light by focusing your consciousness and attention on this source or on building your Lightbody. Strengthen your central vertical channel to directly interface with and lengthen your antennae, connecting directly to the Universal or God power supply.

Mindful Meditation and Spiritual Practice
Clear your mind through daily meditation and direct your energy towards spiritual practices. This becomes a supportive part of your lifestyle, enhancing your connection to the plasma light source.

12D Shield Practice
The 12D shield is a powerful spiritual practice to help you connect with the plasma light source, building your Lightbody and unlocking your superhero potential.

Superhero Insight: Galactic Gridworkers and Hub Handshakes

Galactic Gridworkers
- **Setting Up Links:** Galactic and Planetary Gridworkers are creating vertical communication links called Hub Handshake fields. These links help Guardian Races connect with Krystal Star families on Earth.

Spinning Vortexes
- **Toroidal Fields:** These links create spinning vortexes that transform into toroidal fields with a neutral core, like the 12D Shield Hub. They manage energy currents and higher frequencies during the Ascension Cycle.

Reconnecting Spiritual Links
- **Hub Handshake:** Christos Starseeds use the Hub Handshake to pierce the NET, reconnecting spiritual links and communicating with Krystal Star and Diamond Sun Christos races.

Resetting Reversal Networks
- **12D Ray:** The 12D Ray's corrected current resets and reprograms Reversal Networks like the Anubian Black Heart systems in the Planetary Grid.

Zero Point Field - *The source of the* <u>Zero Point</u> *field is the infinite energy supply of our God Creator that is contained within all living things.*
- **Cosmic Blueprint:** The Hub Handshake also steps down the Zero Point Field and cosmic Christ intelligence Blueprint into the Collective Consciousness fields, stabilizing the Earth's surface against disasters.

Building the Gridwork
- **Trinity Wave**: After establishing the Hub Handshake, we can lay down the Trinity Wave and Krystal Star architecture for expanding the Triad Communication Station. This helps repair planetary systems and reconnect spiritual links within oneself and the Earth's grid.

Join the Galactic Gridworkers in their mission to establish Hub Handshakes and harmonize Earth's energy grid, unleashing your superhero potential!

From within your 12D Shield, create the Hub Handshake with the Unity Vow:

Defenders of Truth, Sovereignty and Liberation. Guardian Families, serving the One.

- From across all the Multiverses I call upon my Guardian families to join me now.
- My unification is demonstrated in the waves of Omni Love – I sound my heart tone to you now.
- My energy template updated, renewed and forever perpetuated in the Eternally Sustained Light.
- My Alchemical Container is consecrated and dedicated to the Purposes of One, and I endeavor to be the Knower of God to then be the Way Shower of God.
- Please sustain me in the Eternal Power of my Consecration.
- I have asked for your Gatekeeping in order to hold my mission, my highest purpose in Service to the One Light, my Source, the Living Light Code.
- My Intention is Unification – the Cosmic Christ Principle – as an Energetic Reality, here and now.
- I request the handshake to fortify my spiritual links through the Universal Cosmic Trinity, and into the Core of One, the Zero Point God Matrix, that which is the source of my Genesis.
- With deep reverence for all of Life, Dear God, Breathe your living life codes into my created form.
- I set my intention now to be remembered to that which I AM, fully, completely and totally, God Sovereign Free!

I state my mutual purpose as One, please resurrect all inorganic and artificial patterns to the Organic Living Light now. And to that I say, Thank God I AM the Living Eternal Light.

Conscious Attunement

- For those new to the 12D Shield and the "Unity Vow," repeat this command with every meditation to entrain your field and create the Hub Handshake hub of direct communication with the Unity Field intelligence of the Krystal Star.
- When feeling the need to strengthen or amplify your communication links, repeat this Unity Vow.
- When proficient with meditation and energy session work, and by holding down the containment field, the Unity Vow becomes entrained with your nervous system, brain and blood, by simply saying "Unity". This statement of intention will sufficiently activate the Hub Handshake to Krystal Star.

**Refer to energeticsysnthesis.com

12D Hub Superhero Activation

In the name of the One Self God Self, Beloved Guardians of Cosmic Christ Light, aligned with the Aurora Platform and the Sacred Law of One:

- I AM *Unity*!
- Activate your 12D Super Shield!

Ignite Your Light:
- Imagine a spark of pale silver light glowing in your pineal gland. Exhale it rapidly toward the Earth's 12D Frequency Hub. See the hub spinning powerfully!

Connect the Cord:
- Visualize a pale silver cord stretching from the Earth's hub, wrapping around you in a luminous shield. Send it soaring out to deep space, anchoring to the Star of Pale Aqua Blue Light.

Call for Guardians:
- Invite the Ascension Teams, Christos Starseed Forces, and Higher Selves to amplify infinite love, light, and power.

Expand the 12D Field:
- Activate a vortex of platinum-white light spinning counterclockwise.
- Grid the entire space with this light.
- Lock in the calibration, anchor, and seal the hologram.

Seal Your Super Space:
- Command the Krystal Compass: North, South, East, West—Earth, Sky, Heart.
- Seal the Four Corners in Unity Light.
- Anchor with Aurora Forces, declaring: "I AM Sovereign, I AM Invincible!"

Claim Your Power:
- Declare your divine inheritance, align with patterns of perfection for all beings, and affirm:
  - "I AM the Diamond Sun! I AM the 12D Light expanding outward in unity!"

Recalibrate and Align:
- Synchronize with Aurora Earth Frequency Hubs.
- Align your channels to Krysthala and Aurora's divine energies.
- Harmonize and hold this space in the name of Wholeness and Union.

** Special thanks to Lisa Renee @ EnergeticSynthesis.com

Seal the Meditation:
- Lock in the Light of One through all dimensions, timelines, and energy systems. Affirm:
- "This space is Sovereign, Sacred, and Anchored in Eternal Light."

12D Super Shield: Activating the Transit Gate

Once you master working with your 12D Shield daily, your Lightbody aligns with the powerful 12D Ray. This alignment forms the spiritual foundation for your Soul, Monad, and Avatar bodies—your ascension arsenal. At higher levels of proficiency, the 12D Shield becomes more than just a protective field—it transforms into a **Transit Gate Vortex**, or Shadow Gate, designed to clear low-vibration energies, entities, and negativity from your space.

- This is your Command Center of Sovereignty, powered by the God-Sovereign-Free Triad—aligned with the Sacred Law of One and the Christ Force. You are the guardian of your personal space, declaring your authority and choosing the light of unity.

Using the 12D Shield as a Shadow Vortex
- Activate your 12D Portal by visualizing it spinning outward in glowing concentric circles, expanding with radiant energy around you. From this portal, you'll create a Transit Gate Vortex—a cosmic doorway that clears and transitions shadow energies.

The Shadow Vortex Protocol
Step 1:
- Call in your support team from the Starseed Families of Oneness.
- "I open this session in service to the Law of One. As I am God, Sovereign, and Free, I so decree:"

Step 2: Bless the Space
- Generate a Field of Divine Grace around this room, land, or location.
- Anchor frequencies of Unconditional Love and Forgiveness here.
- Bless all beings, human and non-human, in the Light of One Source God.
- **Declare:** "I claim this space and all beings in my care as Sovereign and Free, now and always. Seal these blessings into permanent installation here."

Step 3: Set the Shadow Vortex
- Designate a specific space (e.g., the east corner of the room):
- "I request assistance to create a vortex here, serving as an exclusive exit point for all shadow elements."

Command the clearance:
- "All shadow elements within myself, others, and all beings, plants, animals, spaces, and dimensions surrounding me are to exit through this Transit Gate Vortex."

Thank the energies:
- "I thank all shadow elements for transitioning through this gateway. This space is now sealed, Sovereign, and Free in the Light of God."

When we incarnate on Earth, our DNA contains genetic time codes connected to the Planetary Gates, which form our Human Tribal Identity. By activating our Inner Christos with the 12D Ray, we string 144 harmonics throughout our Lightbody, creating the 12D Shield. This identity has experienced many lifetimes, participating in the evolution of DNA codes in the angelic human Root Races across the Solar System.

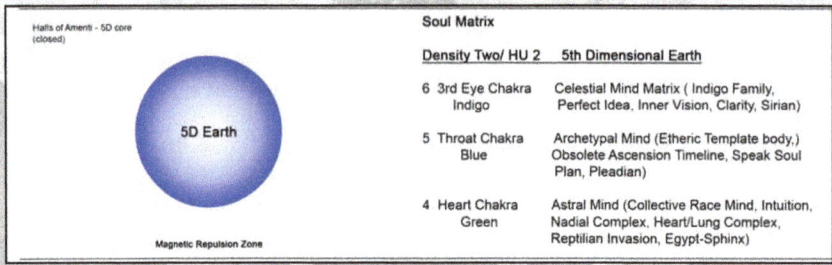

Superhero Soul Integration

Unlock Your Multidimensional Powers
Soul and Monad:
- Your Superfamily of Consciousness
- Your Soul and Monad are like a superhero family, with extensions existing in different dimensions and timelines.

First Level of Awakening
- The first step in your spiritual journey is connecting with your soul consciousness and its extensions.
- Your soul family includes 12 unique personalities.
- As you integrate these aspects, your consciousness body unifies, and you start experiencing emotions and love in powerful new ways.

Complete Soul Integration
- Reaching full soul integration takes you to the next level—integrating with your Monadic or Oversoul Matrix.
- This matrix contains 12 oversouls, each with 12 souls, totaling 144 extensions.
- Each stage of integration significantly expands your consciousness, connecting you to everything and revealing a Universe filled with endless possibilities.

Accelerated Integration
- Right now, the process of soul extension and monadic family reintegration is happening faster than ever, thanks to the shift into organic timelines.

At the time of full monadic body integration, the chakra membranes dissolve, and the lightbody structure begins to change into an orb body that accretes the source field or Plasma waves.

When we energetically evolve and move up in dimensional frequency bands, we are exposed to more dimensional octaves, therefore more potential timelines.

The monadic core is a fascinating aspect of our spiritual anatomy, situated in the thymus area and resonating with the 8th-dimensional chakra. When this dimension begins to activate, it triggers a remarkable transformation within our heart's crystalline structure, fundamentally altering its function.

Key Points to Illuminate

Planetary and Galactic Layers
- **Planetary Layers (1-7):** These layers are intimately connected to the energies of our planet, grounding us in the physical and emotional realms.
- **Galactic Layers (8 and above):** As we ascend beyond the 7th layer, we tap into galactic energies. These layers connect us to multiple bodies across other planets and star systems, expanding our consciousness beyond Earth.

The Monadic 8th Dimension
- The 8th dimension, known as the monadic level, is a gateway to profound changes. This dimension is harmonized with the mother energy, a nurturing and transformative force.
- As the monadic core activates, it influences our biorhythms and the production of certain heart-related chemicals, creating a symphony of energetic and physical transformations.

Crystalline Heart Transformation
The activation of the monadic core initiates the crystallization of the heart, turning it into a beacon of higher vibrations and light.
This crystalline structure enhances our ability to love unconditionally, connect with higher realms, and embody divine energies.

The Transformation of the Heart Chakra
The monad, encompassing the 7th, 8th, and 9th layers, begins to connect at the 8th chakra level, which is the higher heart. Here's the exciting transformation:
- **Heart Chakra Changes** As the monad activates, the heart chakra transforms from an astral heart to a blue heart. The energy frequency flowing through turns blue.
- **Blue Connection** This blue heart connects to the turquoise energy of the mother, something entirely new and profound. (HOLY SPIRIT)
- **8th Dimension** While the 8th dimension is typically gold, the flowering monad in the heart turns it blue, known as the living lotus.

144 SOUL EXTENSIONS - SUPERHEROES

Imagine your soul as a radiant star, connected to a vast network of other stars. This network is your Monad, or your divine spark.

- Each Monad is made up of 12 souls, and each of these souls has 12 soul extensions. Together, this forms a grand total of 144 soul extensions.
- These soul extensions are like different facets of your spiritual self, each representing unique aspects of your consciousness and experiences. As you journey through life and spiritual growth, you connect with these extensions, integrating them into your being. This process helps you to unlock higher levels of awareness and connect with the greater universal consciousness.
- Think of it as a beautiful, intricate web of light, with each thread representing a soul extension. As you weave these threads together, you create a harmonious and balanced spiritual tapestry, illuminating your path to enlightenment.

Understanding Your Chakras and Spiritual Journey
Chakras and Soul Connection

Chakras: Energy centers in our body, each connected to different aspects of our being and higher dimensions.

First Level (Ego/Personality): 1st, 2nd, 3rd Chakras: Represent the ego and personality.

Second Level (Soul Identity)
- 4th Chakra (Heart): Connects us to our soul family.
- 5th Chakra (Throat): Represents communication and truth.
- 6th Chakra (Third Eye): Linked to intuition and insight.

Transitioning Beyond Ego Moving beyond the ego involves shifting from the 1st, 2nd, and 3rd chakras to the soul level (4th, 5th, and 6th chakras).

Oversoul and Planetary Mind - 7th Chakra and Beyond:
- Connects to the oversoul energy and planetary mind level.
- Allows access to higher consciousness and planetary memory.

Ascension Journey
- We are on an accelerated path of ascension, with various levels of initiation based on our Lightbody and soul agreements.
- Recognizing ourselves as spiritual beings, we work with the seven main chakras to achieve planetary ascension.

Liberation and Universal Plan
- Integrating the seven chakras frees us from the reincarnation cycle.
- Connects us to the Universal divine plan and deeper understanding of Earth's purpose.

Uniting 144 Souls Meditation: The Epic Adventure to Unite 144 Superheroes from Your Soul Family

Prepare for the Mission
Find Your Hero Lair: Settle into a serene, quiet space where you feel at ease. Sit or lie down comfortably and take a few deep breaths, letting your mind and body relax as you prepare for this epic mission.

Step-by-Step Superhero Meditation
Set Your Intention
- Begin by setting your intention to connect with your monadic family and all 143 other soul extensions.
- Silently or aloud, affirm your desire for unity and spiritual evolution. Imagine you're about to assemble your superhero team, ready to conquer the cosmos!

Heart Connection
- Shift your awareness to your heart chakra, feeling its warmth and love.
- Visualize a brilliant light emanating from your heart, expanding outward like a beacon guiding your fellow superheroes.

Call in Your Soul Family
- With a loving and open heart, call upon your monadic family.
- Visualize 143 luminous superheroes appearing around you, each representing a soul extension.
- Feel their presence and the deep connection you share, like reuniting with your cosmic Justice League.

Unite and Collaborate
- Imagine a golden light linking each soul extension to you and to one another, creating a powerful web of unity.
- Invite them to join you on this journey of spiritual evolution.
- Mentally communicate your desire for collaboration and intersection at the higher selves' level, like forming an intergalactic superhero alliance.

Elevate Your Consciousness
- Visualize a column of light ascending from your heart, reaching up through your crown chakra and into the higher realms.
- See this light connecting to a vast, cosmic consciousness, embodying the collective wisdom of your entire monadic family.
- Feel the energies blending harmoniously, elevating your consciousness to superhero levels.

Anchor the Unity
- Allow the golden light to flow back down through your chakras, anchoring this unified energy into your being. Sense the integration of your multidimensional aspects, all working together in perfect harmony, like the ultimate superhero team.

Reflect and Journal
- When you feel ready, gently bring your awareness back to the present moment.
- Take a few deep breaths, grounding yourself in the here and now.
- Reflect on your experience and document your feelings and insights in your superhero journal.

Affirm Your Unity
- Affirm that you are now aligned with your monadic family and committed to your collective spiritual evolution.
- Repeat a positive affirmation such as, "I am united with my soul family, and together we ascend to higher realms of consciousness."

This meditation is a powerful tool to connect and collaborate with your soul extensions, fostering a deep sense of unity and accelerating your spiritual growth. Embrace the magic of this process and trust in the profound transformation it brings. (Cape optional, superhero spirit essential!)

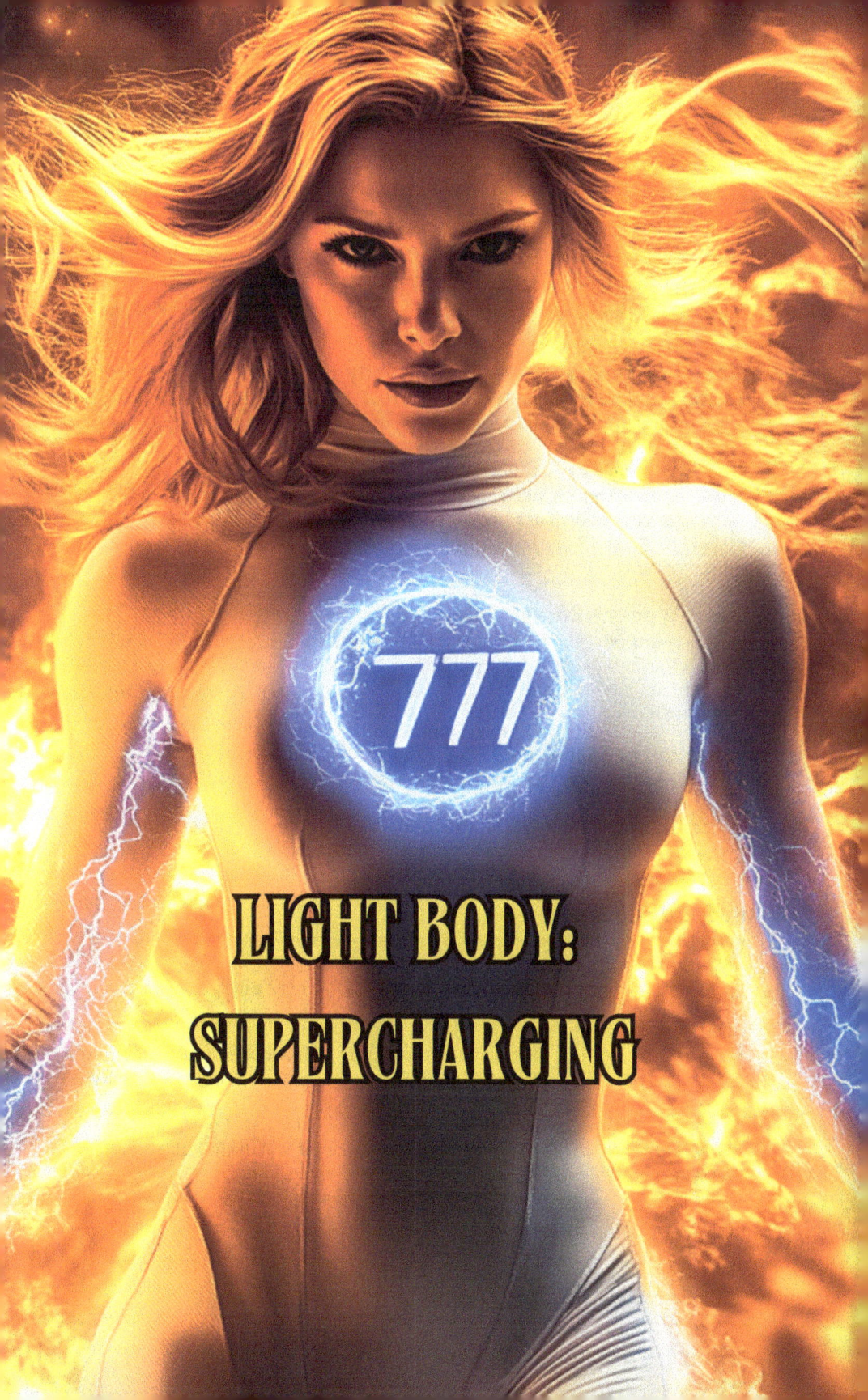

Supercharging Your Lightbody: The Ultimate Superhero Guide

- Your Lightbody is your energy field, like an invisible superhero suit that projects your consciousness and powers.
- This suit generates the physical world you experience, powered by layers of light and sound waves that make up your consciousness across different dimensions in the Universal Time Matrix.
- It's your energy blueprint, holding your identity and connecting you directly to your higher self and the Source.

3 Levels of Your Superhero Lightbody

- **Level 1: *12 Tree Grid and Horizontal Triad Bodies*:** Imagine your first layer as a powerful grid structure, forming the foundation of your superhero energy system.
- **Level 2: *Chakra Crystal Keys, Axiatonal Lines, Hara and Nadial Structure*:** The second layer includes special crystal keys and lines that channel energy through your body like a high-tech power grid.
- **Level 3: *Chakra System*:** Your third layer is the chakra system, the core energy centers that keep you balanced and supercharged.

How It Works - Energy Shield:

- Your Lightbody surrounds you like a protective energy shield, keeping your consciousness body safe and strong.
- When you meditate and practice 12D Shielding, you're boosting this shield, making it even more powerful.

Connection to Soul-Spirit:

- The Lightbody is essential for connecting your soul and spirit to your physical body.
- Electrical impulses from the Lightbody (through the Nadial Structure) link your soul-spirit to your brain and nerves, ensuring seamless communication.

Mind-Body Link:

- These impulses help build new neural networks in your brain, instructing your mind and spirit to grow your energy field.
- This forms your aura, which projects your superhero energy outward.

Aura Health:

- The color, size, and brightness of your aura reflect your overall health and balance. Refer to **Ascension Classified Intel** Book, Aura Section, pages 106-119,
- A bigger, brighter aura = a more powerful and balanced superhero.
- Small, gray, cloudy auras can cause issues like mental dysfunction or brain and nerve problems.
- Embrace your Lightbody, supercharge your aura, and unleash your full superhero potential!

Your invisible suit of power awaits!

Crystalline Superpowers: Unleash Your Inner Hero

- Just like Earth, our bodies and DNA are made of crystalline properties. Imagine yourself as a superhero with a crystalline blueprint called the Silicate Matrix DNA.
- This gets activated when you connect with love-coded hydroplasmic light, which is like liquid crystals.

Your Crystalline Energy Field:

- **Energy Centers**: Your energy field is made up of oscillating centers nested in a multi-dimensional blueprint of crystals.
- **Piezoelectric Properties**: From your organs to your bones, your body parts have piezoelectric (crystal-like) properties. Your bones, the solid crystals, act as the main frequency transducers.

Superhero Powers:

- **Energy Shield**: Your energy field acts like a protective shield, organizing into crystalline functions that keep you strong and balanced.
- **Amplify, Absorb, Store, Transmit**: Like a crystal, you can amplify, absorb, store, and transmit vibrational energies. This impacts your overall health and balance.

How to Harness Your Superpowers:

- **Sustain Life Force**: Keep your life force circulating through your crystalline structure. This ensures you stay energetically balanced and healthy.
- **Crystalline Awareness**: Be aware of your crystalline nature and how it allows you to conduct energy. Everything you encounter has an energetic signature affecting your balance.

Embrace your crystalline superpowers and become the superhero you were meant to be!

Your inner hero awaits!

Superpowered Understanding of Your Lightbody

Awareness of Your Lightbody
- Imagine yourself as a superhero! Your Lightbody is your energy field, a powerful suit made of pure energy and vibration.
- Everything around and within you is an energetic form with its own frequency.

15 Wave Spectrum of Frequency
- In your superhero training, you recognize and work with 15 Wave Spectrum of Frequency.
- These correlate with the Universal Rays and your individual Chakra systems, helping you harness cosmic energy.
- The 12D SUPER WHITE Ray is like the ultimate power-up! It's a white ray (an electromagnetic wave) that represents a level of our being known as the Avatar Christos, manifesting in the 12th dimension of the Universal Time Matrix. In *Ascension Classified Intel* and *5D Ascension Journal*, I provided the 12D shield from Energeticsynthesis.com (I use this 12D shield DAILY).
- Remember the 12D WHITE RAY encompasses all the colors of the spectrum!!
- Understanding and working with these frequencies boosts your superhero powers, helping you connect deeply with your higher self and the universe.

Pure Energy and Consciousness
- As a superhero, you are made of pure energy and consciousness. The way you express emotions, thoughts, memories, and experiences shapes your physical reality.
- By mastering this, you become a powerful and responsible manifestor, creating joy and fulfillment in your world.

Axiatonal Lines - These are like your superhero power lines! Each Axiatonal Line corresponds to a dimension, Chakra, chakra crystal, and frequency color.
- Right Hand: Male, Transmitter, Electric, Clockwise Rotation (3-6-9-2-8, from Right to Left)
- Left Hand: Female, Receiver, Magnetic, Counter-Clockwise Rotation (4-7-10-1-5, from Left to Right)

By understanding and harnessing your Lightbody, you unlock your full superhero potential, connecting deeply with your higher self and the universe.

Your cosmic powers await!

Superhero Insight: Axiatonal Lines and Chakra Power

Level Two Lightbody

- **Axiatonal Lines:** These mighty frequency lines charge through the Chakra Crystal Keys, forming 12 Vertical Lines that funnel cosmic energy to your chakras.
- They intersect with the Horizontal Triad Bodies, creating powerful energy points where your superhero DNA manifests.

Chakra Crystal Keys

- The rotational spin of these keys on the Hara Line acts like a cosmic control panel, modulating frequencies and intelligence through the Axiatonal Lines, supercharging your chakras and body systems.
- The crystal seals grid keeps the particle spin and frequency levels in check, ensuring smooth energy transmission into the chakra.
- This rotation maintains the balance of different identities and dimensions, keeping your superhero auric layers in harmony.

12 Axiatonal Lines
Level Two Lightbody

- Each Axiatonal Line is a corresponding dimension, chakra, chakra crystal and the frequency color
- These 12 vertical Lines create intersection points with the horizontal fields that project out the Chakra cone and where the DNA manifest
- Crucifixion Implants, though DNA mutation placed on 7D Female Left Side Axiatonal Lines
- Personal and Planetary DNA damage with 7D Ray, Axiatonal Lines, Ley Lines from Planetary Mind /Logos Invasion
- Crucifixion Initiation happens at 7D Monadic Body, remove implants possible

4 7 10 15	11 12	8 2 9 6 3
Left Side Female	Hara Line Unity	Right Side Male

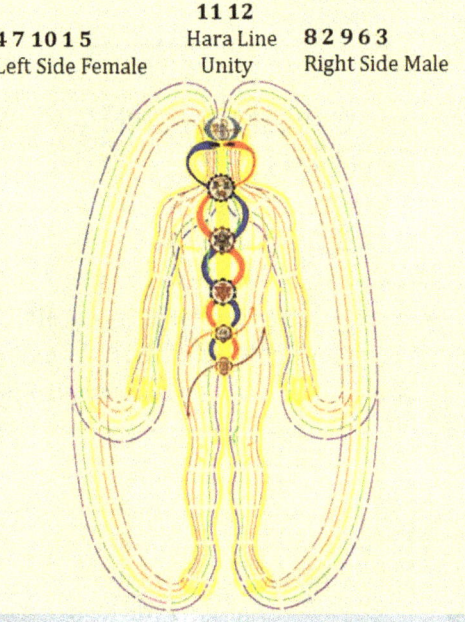

**http://www.energeticsynthesis.com

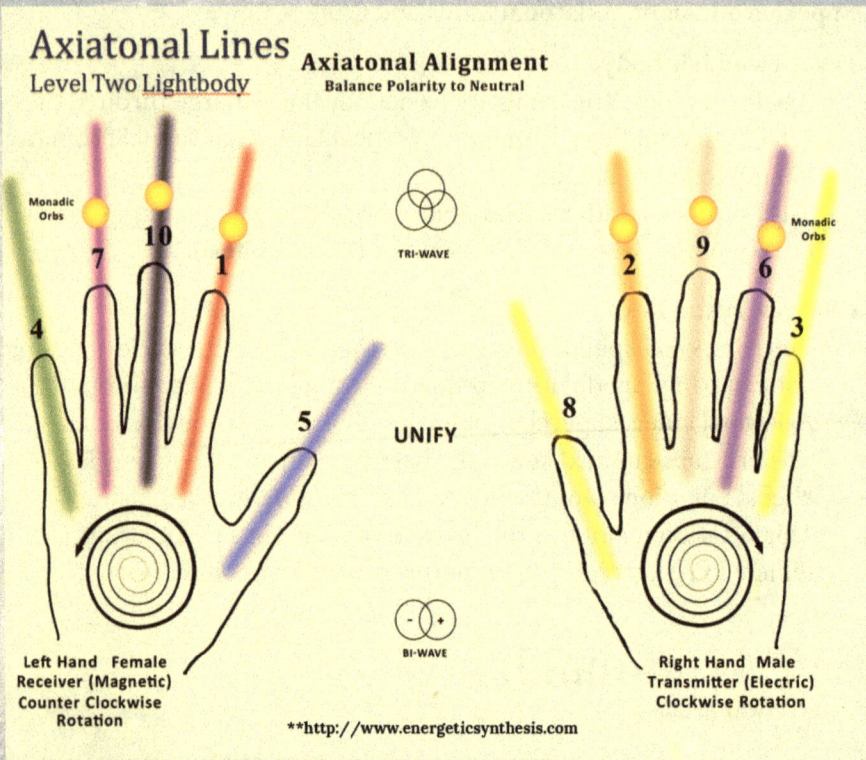

Superhero Insight: Axiatonal Lines and Energy Alignment

Axiatonal Lines
- Axiatonal Lines form the energy network in your Lightbody, channeling dimensional frequencies into meridians, chakras, and the etheric structure.
- There are 12 vertical lines running energy to the chakras, intersecting with horizontal fields that project from the Chakra cones where DNA manifests. Each line corresponds to a dimension, chakra, crystal, and frequency color.

Energy Rotation
- Left Hand: Female, Receiver, Magnetic, Counter-Clockwise (4-7-10-1-5 from Left-Right).
- Right Hand: Male, Transmitter, Electric, Clockwise (3-6-9-2-8 from Right-Left).

Central Hara Line: Unity (11-12, straight up and down).

Axiatonal Alignment

- This alignment secures vertical connections, calibrating your energy network to support maximum health, harmony, and energetic balance.
- It's a crucial step to connect with your inner core, part of the energetic HGS Calibration process.

Calibration Protocol
Step One Calibration Step One Axiatonal Alignment and Correction of Reversal Polarities in Aura

- Place Right and Left hand on Top of Hands in Graphic Aid Close Eyes and Intend to Induct Code and Unify Polarity.
- State the Axiatonal Alignment in the Numerical Order as on the Chart Left to Right, Right to Left to meet in Center Point as Neutral To entrain the code:
  - State the command "Axiatonal Alignment 4-7-10-1-5 Left. Axiatonal Alignment 3-6-9-2-8 Right. UNIFY!"
- If you are upset, frustrated or excessively tired this will not hold Either correct zero point/neutral observer to conditions or stop session.
- Hydrate with some water Stretch, walk around or reposition 12D Shield helps to create neutral balance.

Harness the power of Axiatonal Lines to supercharge your energy network and achieve peak performance on your superhero journey!

- Krystallah Lightbody Activating the Diamond Sun Body in 5D merges male-female energy spirals into a large orb of light.
- This creates three main orb bodies aligned in the central Vertical Channel, leading to the Personal Christ at the 12th Sphere.
- These orb bodies merge into a non-polarized energy center.

Superhero's Guide to the Merkaba and Lightbody
- Your consciousness units are like superhero building blocks, arranging into dimensional grids that form layers of energy fields. These fields contain specific instructions that build energy spirals, creating the Merkaba fields.

Merkaba Fields
- The Merkaba fields sustain the energy that builds your entire Lightbody.
- Think of them as your superhero power source, with male-female sets of counter-rotating electromagnetic spirals of consciousness energy.
- These spirals generate a DNA and RNA imprint—DNA being the masculine principle and RNA the feminine. They must work together in balance, like a superhero duo.

Auric Field
- Your auric field is made up of multiple layers of energy matrices, acting like small computers. These are your chakras.
- The lower chakras exist in particle layers, while the higher dimensional chakras exist in anti-particle layers.
- Anti-particle chakras, also called Morphogenetic Chakras, provide instruction sets to the lower dimensional chakras, helping you unlock higher frequencies over time.

Nadial Capsule
- Chakras send processed energy as intelligent spirals into the nadial capsule, which forms around your physical body.
- It's like your superhero suit, guiding how your consciousness organizes into DNA and RNA.
- The Nadial Capsule instructs how to manifest this energy into your physical form, creating a blueprint for your brain and nervous system.

Central Nervous System
- Your central nervous system transmits energy from your DNA and RNA into the molecular structure, then into the nuclear core of your Atomic Body, informing the Dark Matter Template.
- This core sends intelligent energy into your central nervous system, setting your metabolic and biological rhythms.

Blood and Hormones
- These rhythms, imprinted by your soul and spiritual intelligence, form historical records in your blood. These records help produce and distribute hormones, affecting every organ and gland in your body.

By understanding the interaction of these elements, you harness your unique consciousness and spiritual records, becoming the ultimate superhero with a fully powered Lightbody.

SELF-HEALING IS CRUCIAL

- Self-healing and learning to love ourselves enables us to reclaim our true selves and love others more freely.
- To love others without fear, we must first be at peace and in love with ourselves.
- Self-esteem, dignity, and self-respect open us to loving others selflessly. This is the journey we are on at the end of the Ascension Cycle—to become truly human again.

Make a choice right now which thoughts you want to own and those you want to discard.

- As a goal use the above spiritual self-centering model to keep your mind balanced and stay in centered loving and neutral thoughts. How long can you stay there in the center?

We are in the process of dissolving our EGO, it is daily work and acknowledgement

- Superior Thinking: Intolerance, Impatience, Arrogance, Manipulation, Attack, Anger, Judgmental thinking
- Inferior Thinking: Worry, Low Self Love or Esteem, Jealousy, Guilt, Hurt, Fear, Attachment, Martrydom

This is an exhilarating time of transformation, where the boundaries of reality are expanding, and we're stepping into our multidimensional potential.

- Embrace these changes, knowing that every energetic upgrade is bringing you closer to a higher state of existence. The adventure of ascension is truly unfolding, and it's an incredible journey to be part of!
- Understanding the structure of your being is key to spiritual healing. Think of it as becoming your own spiritual illuminator, performing Etheric Surgery.

Integrating Your Etheric Body: An Exciting Transformation
For those who have embarked on a journey of inner healing and detoxification, a remarkable transformation is taking place. Your physical body is now absorbing and integrating your etheric body. Here's what this means, and why it's so exciting:

Harmonizing Physical and Etheric Energies
- **Energetic Synergy** Your physical body and etheric body are merging into one harmonious unit, enhancing your overall energy and vitality.
- **Higher Vibrations** This integration elevates your vibrational frequency, aligning you with higher states of consciousness and spiritual awareness.

Enhanced Healing and Vitality
- **Cellular Activation** Your cells are becoming more attuned to higher energies, promoting healing and rejuvenation at a deeper level.
- **Increased Vitality** As your body integrates these etheric energies, you may experience a surge in energy, clarity, and overall well-being.

Greater Spiritual Awareness
- **Heightened Intuition**: Your connection to your higher self and spiritual guides becomes stronger, enhancing your intuition and inner knowing.
- **Deeper Insights**: You gain access to greater spiritual insights and wisdom, helping you navigate life's challenges with ease and grace.

Empowered Manifestation
- **Creative Power** With your energies aligned, your ability to manifest your desires and goals becomes more potent and effective.
- **Synchronicity** You begin to notice an increase in synchronicities and meaningful coincidences, indicating that you are in harmony with the universe.

Emotional Liberation:
- **Release of Blockages**: The integration process helps release emotional blockages and past traumas, freeing you from limiting patterns and beliefs.
- **Inner Peace**: You experience a profound sense of inner peace and emotional balance, allowing you to live more authentically and joyfully.

Embrace the Transformation
This integration is a sign of your spiritual progress and evolution. By harmonizing your physical and etheric bodies, you are stepping into a new realm of potential and enlightenment. Embrace this exciting journey, knowing that you are becoming a more empowered, vibrant, and spiritually attuned version of yourself. The future is bright, and your transformation is unfolding beautifully!

An Exciting Journey: Chakra Balance Through the Hara Line
Get Comfortable
- Imagine yourself gearing up for an epic adventure. Sit with your spine straight, close your eyes, and take a few deep, calming breaths.
- Inhale deeply through your nose, hold for a moment, and exhale slowly through your mouth. Feel your body relax as you prepare for this journey.
- Focus on Your Hara Line.
- Visualize a glowing line of energy starting two inches below your navel. This is your Hara line. See it as a radiant pathway of light running straight down into the earth and extending upward through your body.
- Dive Into the Earth
- Shift your focus downward along the Hara line, imagining it as a magical tunnel diving deep into the earth. As you travel downward, check for any blockages or imbalances in the energy flow. Does it feel clear and grounded? Picture yourself exploring an enchanted cavern, ensuring everything flows smoothly.

Ascend to the Stars
- Now, shift your focus upward along the Hara line, traveling through your body and up toward the crown of your head.
- As you ascend, check if the energy feels balanced and free-flowing. Are any areas of your chakras blocked or weak?
- Visualize yourself rising into the cosmos, aligning with the stars.

Restore the Balance
- If you encounter any blockages or imbalances, visualize a bright, cleansing light flowing through those areas, clearing and balancing the energy. Feel the flow of energy being restored through the entire Hara line. Imagine yourself as a powerful sorcerer, casting a spell of harmony and balance.
- Take a Final Deep Breath
- Take a deep breath, feeling the alignment and balance throughout your entire body. When you're ready, gently open your eyes, feeling centered and harmonious. You've completed your journey, returning with newfound clarity and peace.
- Embark on this exciting meditation journey anytime you need to check and balance your chakras. It's a magical adventure within, leading you to a state of perfect harmony and alignment.

Superhero's Guide to Chakra Mastery
- Balancing and clearing your chakras daily is crucial—it's like polishing your superhero armor. If you're not basking in the sun and grounding yourself with Earth's energy, embracing your higher consciousness will be a lot tougher. The sun is your cosmic power source, supercharging your abilities.
- In my book, *Ascension Classified Intel*, I've included the ultimate starseed supplement and a ton of lower chakra troubleshooting techniques. Think of it as your superhero manual for unlocking and maintaining your full potential.

Remember, superheroes, keeping those chakras aligned and powered up is the key to unlocking your cosmic consciousness and living your best superpowered life.

Superhero Insight: Cosmic Lightbody Upgrades
Seven Suns Frequencies
- The Seven Suns frequencies create a new base shield template, replacing the old 3D grounding mechanism in the lower chakras and Earth interface. This new template is called the Base 360 Grounding Shield, providing a Non-Polarized Base Shield that can access any timeline.

Base 360 Grounding Shield
- This shield means the lightbody's core is in no-time, with Transharmonic ability to enter any timeline. It builds the Eukachristic Body for Avatar Christos-Sophia consciousness, leading to the Krystallah eternal lightbody, a unified male-female expression.

Superhero Insight: Unlocking Higher Senses

Awakening Higher Senses - SUPERPOWERS
- Many higher senses go unrecognized as normal traits of a spiritually awakened human.
- These senses may activate when someone advances to higher spiritual frequencies.
- Individuals showcasing these abilities are not especially gifted; they simply represent the future potential of humanity's activated DNA.

DNA and Higher Senses - SUPERPOWERS
- Higher Sensory Perception and all senses are governed by DNA. Those with an open-heart center and fewer distortions in their personal Blueprint find it easier to activate these dormant abilities.

Belief and Activation
- If a person rejects the idea that higher sensory perception is a normal function of human DNA, they will shut off these abilities completely.
- As Earth shifts to the next harmonic, the population is exposed to 4D-5D-6D incoming Soul frequency patterns, activating a new set of higher sensory abilities.

Self-Study
- Self-Study is the path to self-mastery.
- By expanding our consciousness, we naturally enhance all functions of our Higher Sensory Perception.

Mastering the Mind
- Consistent meditation is a powerful tool for training an undisciplined and cluttered mind.
- It helps develop higher consciousness, paving the way for Higher Sensory Perception.
- Without a trained and disciplined mind, developed HSP is unlikely for most people.

Meditation Techniques
- Meditation can be practiced in many ways, all helpful for facilitating forgiveness and letting go of negativity.

Superhero Insight: Unlocking Cellular Telepathy

Beyond Mental Knowledge
- Expanding consciousness transcends linear thinking and enters the realm of Direct Knowing and Cellular Telepathy, natural functions of our spiritual biology.
- Cellular telepathy means every cell in your body is alive and intelligent, allowing messages and thoughts to be transmitted without the brain or mind.

Direct Knowing
- Suspend linear thought and mental chatter to be fully present, observing and feeling the energy around you. This practice allows your higher senses to activate, letting intelligent energies give your cells impressions and information without words.
- As you breathe deeply, feel the energy signature around you. This practice activates your higher senses, allowing your body to receive impressions and information without words. When you remain present, higher knowing is always within reach.
- Embrace the power of Direct Knowing and step into your superhero potential, fully attuned to the present moment!

Nature's Wisdom
- Stand alone in nature, breathe deeply, and observe the present moment. Connect to the Earth's energies and notice how impressions flood into your awareness.
- The more open your mind and heart, the easier it is to perceive this information.

Cellular Telepathy Activation
- Cellular telepathy strengthens when the soul layers are healed, unified, and connected within the body.
- The Soul Matrix, the first spiritual triad, starts the process of Awakening. When these bodies merge through lightbody activation, new sensory perception functions are activated.

Enteric Nervous System (2nd Brain)
- The 2nd Brain is a network of neurons in your digestive system, acting as a second brain.
- It processes energies, emotions, and sensory experiences, aiding in intuition and awareness.
- A healthy ENS supports brain function, stabilizes moods, and enhances wellbeing.

Overcoming Challenges
- Natural telepathy and empathy come online during soul integration and bio-spiritual healing.
- However, external attempts to control our Bio-Neurology can interfere.
- Recognize that cellular telepathy is inherent to consciousness communication, shaping how our cells organize and manifest our reality.

Embrace your superhero potential by unlocking Cellular Telepathy and tapping into the wisdom of your spiritual biology!

Superhero Insight: The Power of Mirror Neurons
Mirror Neurons
- Your brain contains Mirror Neurons that reflect others' perceptions and responses.
- These neurons read energetic information from another's mind and relay it through your central nervous system, generating feelings of empathy.

Empathy and Psychopathy
- When people are disconnected from their heart and soul, they lose the function of empathy, which can lead to psychopathy.
- Empathy allows us to experience others' emotions and intentions, naturally leading to forms of telepathy.

Everyday Telepathy
- Many people experience telepathy daily but may dismiss it as pseudoscience.
- Telepathic communication goes beyond the physical body; it's an inherent function of the Lightbody, activated through Higher Sensory Perception with spiritual development.

Superhero Insight: The Power of Empathy
Inner Stillness
- When we relax into the inner stillness of our being, free from thought, and feel safe enough to allow ourselves to feel deeply, we open the doorway to empathize with others' emotions.

Mirror Neurons
- Mirror neurons fire in our brains and auras, reflecting others' perceptions and responses.
- This empathy process affects the brains and auras of everyone around us, allowing us to embody the quality of empathy.

Empathy and the Soul
- Empathy is a function of our soul, embodying virtues gained through connecting with higher consciousness.
- When we are present and aware, our mirror neurons help us feel what it's like to be in another person's situation, developing loving compassion.

Compassion and Connection
- Compassion and empathy are the cornerstones of love, interconnecting us to all life. By putting ourselves in another person's shoes, we practice empathy and reflect on our own identity and emotional patterns. This self-realization dissolves the sense of separation.

Neural Pathways
- The more we practice self-reflection and empathy, the more mirror neurons we generate, shifting our personal and others' mental maps.

Healing with Mindfulness
- Practicing mindful meditation and embracing higher emotional behaviors like loving kindness, compassion, and peace can heal the human nervous system.
- These practices also help repair and transform disorders formed by past brain patterns.

Embracing Empathy and Telepathy
Empathic Connection
- By tapping into our empathic connection, we can feel the emotions and intentions of those around us.
- This naturally leads to experiencing forms of telepathy.

Everyday Telepathy
- Many people encounter telepathy daily but are often led to dismiss it. Telepathic communication transcends the physical body; it's an inherent function of our Lightbody.

Higher Sensory Perception
- As we develop our spiritual bodies, Higher Sensory Perception functions activate, enhancing our telepathic abilities.

A Message from the Author

As we journey through life, there are moments when the Soul chooses to release the physical body, transitioning from the Earthly plane to continue its evolution in other realms. These transitions—sometimes unfolding as illness, accidents, or other sudden departures—are deeply personal and aligned with each Soul's unique path. Not every journey is meant to culminate in a physical, biological ascension; for some, the next step requires stepping beyond the confines of this earthly form to reach a higher plane of existence.

In witnessing these sacred transitions, we are called to embody Engaged Neutrality, a state of grounded presence and acceptance, coupled with deep Compassion for the Soul's journey and for those left behind. These moments, as difficult as they may seem, are precisely as they need to be.

Many of us are being called to serve as midwives of the spirit—gentle guides for those crossing over and for the families and friends navigating the mysteries of loss. Whether by creating sacred spaces, offering understanding, or simply holding a loving presence, this role is an act of profound service.

Recently, a noticeable shift has opened, presenting Souls with what might feel like an unusual opportunity to choose whether to stay or leave the Earthly plane. These cycles of completion bring with them both clarity and challenge, as we witness loved ones facing illness, unexpected transitions, or sudden departures. While these experiences can be surprising—even shocking—our greatest offering is to remain anchored in peace, holding space for the wisdom of each Soul's divine timing.

If you are among those called to support these transitions, I want to extend my heartfelt gratitude. Your loving service as a bridge between worlds is a gift that brings comfort and understanding during a time of profound transformation.

We are the final generation to inhabit carbon-based bodies, standing at the threshold of an extraordinary transformation. As the last stewards of this form, we are not merely witnesses to change but active participants in the evolution of humanity itself. We are midwives to a new era, guiding the emergence of crystalline consciousness and the awakening of a luminous, higher-dimensional existence.

Our journey marks the culmination of countless lifetimes of growth and preparation, each moment leading us to this pivotal time. Through our presence, intention, and unwavering resilience, we bridge the old and the new — anchoring the crystalline light codes that will reshape what it means to be human.

This transformation is not just physical but deeply spiritual, touching every facet of our being. It is the alchemy of dense matter into pure light, the unlocking of dormant potentials, and the activation of a higher template for humanity. Together, we are weaving a future where clarity, unity, and love reign, laying the foundation for generations to come.

As we embrace this monumental shift, let us honor the sacred task entrusted to us. We are the guardians of this transition, the pioneers of a crystalline dawn, and the bearers of a radiant legacy that will illuminate the path forward for all who follow.

As we close this book together, may you carry this message with you: every Soul's journey is sacred, and through compassion, presence, and love, we honor the unseen threads that connect us all.

I'm honored to be working with Author and friend, Chris Mayer to bring you a Higher Chakra Morphogenetic Journal that will help you document your progress with this ascension.

My biological name is Lisa Renee, and although I am not affiliated with energeticsynthesis.com, I am inspired by their work. I highly encourage everyone to visit energeticsynthesis.com for further studies and resources.

With gratitude and light,
Lisa Renee

SOURCES AND ACKNOWLEDGEMENTS:

This book draws inspiration from and is referenced by the works of Lisa Renee, the resources available on energeticsynthesis.com, and the wisdom of the Galactic Alliance.

www.ingramcontent.com/pod-product-compliance
Lightning Source LLC
Chambersburg PA
CBHW071453150426
43191CB00008B/1328